THE NILE SWIM CLUB OF YEADON

THE NILE SWIM CLUB OF YEADON

•A HISTORY•

ROBERT J. KODOSKY

Welcome by Anthony Patterson Sr., Foreword by Lamont Ferrell

Published by The History Press
Charleston, SC
www.historypress.com

First published 2024

Manufactured in the United States

ISBN 9781467156127

Library of Congress Control Number: 2023946789

Notice: The information in this book is true and complete to the best of our knowledge. It is offered without guarantee on the part of the author or The History Press. The author and The History Press disclaim all liability in connection with the use of this book.

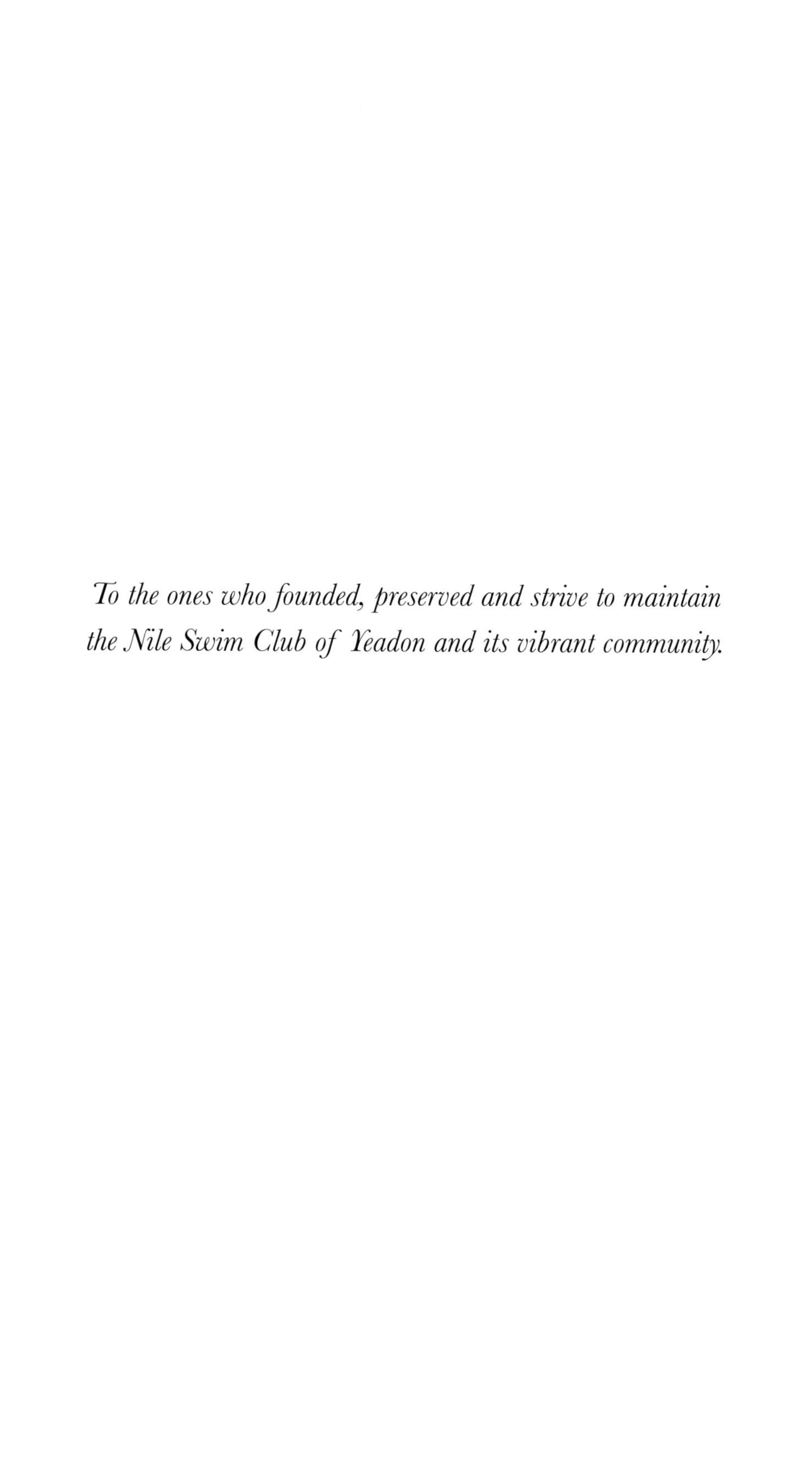

To the ones who founded, preserved and strive to maintain the Nile Swim Club of Yeadon and its vibrant community.

CONTENTS

WELCOME TO
THE NILE SWIM CLUB OF YEADON

My childhood memories revolve around the Nile Swim Club of Yeadon. My dad died when I was three years old. He was a pillar of the community—Reverend Isaac Newton Patterson III. My dad was there at the beginning of the Nile, attending the opening in 1959 with my brothers David and Horace. When my father passed, our family, West Yeadon, felt the loss. But my mother knew that she had to keep our family together. There were fourteen of us at home, and Social Services pressed her to break the family up. My mother, who gave birth to nineteen children, would not let that happen.

My mom went back to school, earned her GED and Nurse's Aid Certification and went to work at Fitzgerald Mercy Hospital. As I grew, I discovered this family nearby, almost right next door, centered around a swimming pool. I knew very little about swimming, but looking through the fence, the crystal blue water, the folks inside, beckoned. Guess I hung out long enough that they invited me inside. That forever changed my life. I discovered the Nile family.

My family could not afford the Niles' membership fees, but everybody seemed to know my dad and siblings. In fact, my oldest brother, Reverend Isaac Patterson IV, was a good friend of Carson Puriefoy, the Nile's first president. A pillar of West Yeadon and the Nile, Mr. Puriefoy and others at the Nile recognized my interest in the club and welcomed me. To my surprise, they let me in! All they required from me was a day's work, picking up trash, scrubbing the pool tiles, helping however I could. In return, I got to swim for the day! And get lunch! Best burger and fries from the Nile's snack bar a child could want. I learned a work ethic at the Nile that stays with me decades later. Moreover, I learned the importance of swimming. I'll never forget the staff, the lifeguards, that helped me learn how to swim and dive, lessons everybody needs, even today—69 percent of our young Black children have little to no swimming capability, and I set out to change that.

While my experience at the club in Yeadon forever shaped me, I left for a time. I went to Cheyney University, one of our nation's premier Historically Black Colleges and Universities (HBCUs), got a Bachelor of Science degree in business administration and marketing and set out to make my mark. I did that, early in the cellular phone business, moving on to develop African American networking opportunities in the Greater Philadelphia area and even working to promote early hip hop icons like Wu-Tang Clan, Biggie Smalls and Naughty By Nature, to name a few. I worked for IBM and my brother Sam's IT consulting firm. I also worked at WDAS and Q102 radio station in sales and marketing, where I mastered my sales skills. My sales experience helped me communicate effectively to negotiate, influence and encourage donor support to raise money for the Nile Swim Club. I later started my own full-service real estate and property management company, which I continue to run.

But the Nile Swim Club of Yeadon remained in my heart, and my heart lead me back to Yeadon. When I saw the Nile decades after I first peered through that fence, I knew I had returned home. But my Nile home needed help. Many of West Yeadon's kids, like me, left town when we grew up. The ones who founded the club, our parents, moved or passed away over time. Membership dipped, and the Nile fell into disrepair and financial distress. It became my mission to restore it. With the help of my family, Kappa Alpha Psi Fraternity Inc., the Nile board and Nile volunteers, many from the neighborhood, we resurrected the club, restoring its mission, rendering it inclusive and broadening its membership and programming.

As the Nile's president, I went to work with the club's community to bring back some of the activities that made the club great when I was a child—such as swimming, basketball, tennis and dancing—and add new features, among them are our flagship program, No Child Will Drown in Our Town™, where children learn to swim for free; the Tennis Academy; the Nile Swim Team; the largest food giveaway in the area, with 2000 boxes distributed every week during the COVID-19 pandemic; and many others. As the first Black swim club in the nation, we were recognized as a Historic Landmark and proudly erected our marker in 2021. The Nile

Swim Club shaped my life, and with the love and support of my wonderful wife, Lori; my son, Anthony Jr.; and my very large family, I am honored to preserve the Nile's legacy and ensure that it gives back all that it gave me. We have much more to do!

Anthony F. Patterson Sr.,
President, Nile Swim Club of Yeadon Board (2019–present)

FOREWORD

When author Robert J. Kodosky asked me to write the foreword for his book, *The Nile Swim Club of Yeadon: A History*, I was elated, honored…and scared to death! I've never written a foreword for a book before. The closest I've got was playing forward at Yeadon/Penn Wood High School and at Temple University on the basketball team. Now, bear in mind I am an award-winning screenwriter, having written for more than a dozen TV shows such as *The Parent 'Hood*, *Moesha*, *Girlfriends*, *House of Payne* and *Are We There Yet?*, just to name a few. But those are TV sitcoms, and I'm a comedy writer—a totally different genre than what Robert has created here. However, despite my fears, I told him yes. Primarily because I admired his work as a historian and a storyteller. He tells the untold stories of people of color that many, quite frankly, would like to forget. Like his book *Tuskegee in Philadelphia: Rising to the Challenge* (The History Press, 2020) for example. In that book, he tells the story about America's Black aviators in the Second World War and the significant role that Philadelphia played in it. This story and countless other like it must be told. The Nile Swim Club of Yeadon is another one of those stories. It's American history. It's our history.

My parents, Willie and Willamae Ferrell (yes, Willie and Willamae; they were made for each other), moved to the suburbs of Yeadon, Pennsylvania, from West Philadelphia in the early '70s to escape gang violence and establish a better life for my five brothers—Terryl, Stephen, Jamar, Jacin and Dion—as well as myself of course. When people heard that a new family moved in with six boys and no girls, the first thing they would say was, "Your poor mother." Moving to Yeadon was like a dream. Even though it was less than thirty minutes from the house in West Philly where we grew up, it was like another world. People didn't lock their doors. The Yeadon Movie Theater was around the corner from our house and only cost a dollar. A dollar! The owner/operator was a little old White woman named Mrs. Freeman who would greet you with a smile, collect your dollar and give you free hot chocolate and candy. The fire station was operated by volunteers. Imagine our surprise when we witnessed many of our neighbors rush out of the house and dash to the firehouse when the fire siren went off. Forget another world—Yeadon was another galaxy. Having a front yard, backyard and long driveway with grass may seem routine to some, but to us it was like an oasis. However, little did we know that the best was yet to come, as the real oasis was just "down the way."

When I first heard of the Nile, I couldn't believe it. "A Black-owned swim club in Yeadon?" I said to myself. Up until that point, many swimming clubs and swimming pools were pretty much off-limits to me and my brothers, as even in the '70s many had the unwritten rule that Blacks weren't allowed. However, this wasn't the case with the Nile. Not only did they embrace us and all people of color, they also welcomed everyone from all races and nationalities. It was five acres of lush parklike setting, tennis courts, basketball courts, playgrounds and, of course, an Olympic-size swimming pool. I can still smell the aroma from the meat grilling from the barbecues, hearing the music blaring from the pool parties blocks away and, of course, being dunked in the pool by my friends. It was like a country club, but the only difference was it was ours.

However, the Nile is much more than a swimming pool. Like it's namesake in northeastern Africa, the Nile flows from the veins of the original clubs' founders into each and every one of us. Robert does an excellent job in his book giving us a historical account and detailed description of their vision and foresight to open their own swim club after being denied membership to the local Yeadon club. It was a testament to who we are as African Americans. Over and over again, when doors are slammed in our faces and the hands of racism and oppression choke us, despite it all, we continue to make a way somehow.

LaMont F. Ferrell,
Writer/Producer/Director,
Screenwriting Professor, University of Southern California (USC),
Instructor, Sundance Collab Institute,
Board Member, Jacobs Film Institute

ACKNOWLEDGEMENTS

Books constitute community efforts, and this one exemplifies that. Thanks to Mel Payne, the director of the Philadelphia Chapter of Tuskegee Airmen. Mel is an advocate of African American history, of American history, and his invitation brought me to the Nile Swim Club of Yeadon. I learned that my visit resulted from the prodding of "Ms." Alma Bailey, a nurse who served in Tuskegee and belongs to the Nile Swim Club. She worked to help save the Nile during its troubled time. Historians reference the World War II generation as America's greatest. From her lifetime of service and the challenges that she successfully negotiated as a Black woman in America, "Ms." Alma Bailey is indeed among the greatest of America's "Greatest Generation." I am fortunate to know her.

Anthony Patterson Sr., president of the Nile Swim Club of Yeadon, met with me and eagerly embraced the idea of writing a book about the Nile's rich history. Anthony is passionate about the Swim Club, its past, present and future. He is enormously optimistic, and his support proved crucial to the completion of this project. Many others from the Nile community also contributed, including Lisa M. Ivery, the Nile's vice-president and one who worked tirelessly to preserve the Nile when it nearly drowned in debt. She offered her stories and photographs and helped interview others. Nile member and Yeadon librarian Cliff "Brother" Brock also helped organize the interviews and provided photos.

This book relies on the stories that so many Nile Swim Club members enthusiastically contributed. I am grateful for their time and for their trust in this process. William Mellix Jr., the son of one of the club's original members, proved instrumental in my effort to tell the Nile's story. He shared with me his collection of historical documents, one that helped him, and the Yeadon Historical Commission, secure a Pennsylvania Historical Marker for the Nile Swim Club. The collection proved an enormous asset to me in telling and contextualizing the Nile's story. Along with others—including Anthony Patterson Sr., Karen Hall Eskridge, Lamont Ferrell and Lisa Ivery—William gave me timely and helpful feedback about this book's drafts.

Many thanks to Denise Stewart Swann and Jacqueline Puriefoy-Brinkley, daughters of Elmer Stewart and Carson Puriefoy, two of the Nile Swim Club's founders. Both shared their experiences with the pool and of growing up in Yeadon with great clarity and insight. Materials that Jacqueline provided me, including her father's original bond certificate, helped me get a true sense of the pride and perseverance of the Nile Swim Club's founding members. A special thanks also goes to Edith "Sugie" Dixon, a stalwart contributor to the club through its history, and William "Bill" Stewart.

From the onset of this project, Dr. Cheri Carter, director of the undergraduate program of social work at Temple University, provided both inspiration and essential insights. She lent her time and expertise generously to the interview process and helped capture the essence of the Nile's community through her photography. Cheri additionally offered feedback about the book's draft and, throughout the project, always asked the right questions. I'm grateful for her collaborative spirit, intellectual rigor and honesty.

While researching, I encountered a story in the *Philadelphia Inquirer* about former Temple University basketball player and acclaimed screenwriter Lamont Ferrell and his ties to the Nile Swim Club. To my surprise, he immediately responded back to my inquiry and proved most generous in his support of this project. I am honored by his willingness to contribute the foreword to this book. Lamont's dedication to remaining connected to his roots at the Nile Swim Club is admirable. I am thankful for his considerable contributions to this project.

I am appreciative of my colleagues, students and administrators at West Chester University. They provide me the space, and the energy, to write history. That is a gift, one that stems from my positive experiences teaching, advising and learning on campus. Much of the writing for this book took place during a five-week break in the summer from serving as department chair. Thank you, Eric Fournier, my amazing assistant chair, and thank you, Jean Bauer, the administrative heart and soul of our department. Time is a precious asset for a writer, and you both ensured that I had it.

This is the second book for me under the direction of Banks Smither, acquisitions editor at The History Press. Banks listened to my pitch and provided me with precisely what I needed to frame it successfully. He anchors this book's community, providing it with ample direction and support. He communicates in a clear and timely way. I hope all who write are as fortunate as I am to work with Banks as my editor. Working with him, along with the rest of his team at The History Press, is a true pleasure.

Thanks to everybody who contributed to telling this story. The merits of the project result from each of your efforts. While I worked to convey the story through your words to the best of my ability, whatever mistakes exist are wholly my own.

INTRODUCTION

How does a White military historian come to write a history about America's oldest Black swim club, the Nile Swim Club of Yeadon? Good question. For much of this country's history, and through its present, there exists a pattern of White historians neglecting, dismissing, marginalizing and altering Black history. Or just getting it wrong, purposely or otherwise. All to support systemic racism. That needs to be acknowledged at the outset, as does the author's positionality. In doing so, this project utilizes the model offered by the late historian Howard Zinn.

In his seminal work, *A People's History of the United States* (Harper & Row, 1980), he cited the "inevitable taking of sides which comes from selection and emphasis in history." Zinn chose the side of America's oppressed and strove to tell their story "to the limited extent that any one person, however he or she strains, can 'see' history from the standpoint of others."

In that spirit, this book conveys the history of the Nile Swim Club of Yeadon, to the extent possible, through the words of the ones who built it, maintained it and forged a community that it continues to inspire. That is my side, the one occupied by the Nile. Its storied past is Black history. That makes it essential to American history. The Nile's story makes manifest President Barack H. Obama's observation about Black cultural expression in "the way that hardship and sorrow were transformed into something full of beauty and vitality and hope."

I became familiar with the Nile's story only after receiving a call in the summer of 2022 from Mel Payne, director of the Philadelphia chapter of Tuskegee Airmen. I worked with Mel a few years before to produce *Tuskegee in Philadelphia: Rising to the Challenge* (The History Press, 2020). In that book, we wanted to tell the story about America's Black aviators in the Second World War. That story is one of people who, because of their skin color, found themselves required to fight for their right to fight for their country. In a war against racism abroad, the men and women of Tuskegee battled segregation and discrimination at home, all to get into the fight. This included not only the unit's pilots but also its mechanics, engineers and nurses who additionally combatted sexism. After many of them contributed substantially to the victory overseas, with great dignity and resolve, they went to work to secure a "Double Victory" by ending racism in America.

One of the individuals featured in *Tuskegee in Philadelphia*, Tuskegee nurse Ms. Alma Bailey, as it turned out, belonged to the Nile Swim Club. Through Mel, she expressed interest in me telling the Nile's story, and I agreed to meet with Nile Swim Club president Anthony Patterson Sr. On a bright sunny day in July, I met Anthony and Mel at the pool. We talked about the Tuskegee book, with all of its proceeds going to a scholarship fund, and agreed easily that we would do the same with this project. Because of systemic economic inequalities, an alarming number of African Americans drown annually. In some small way, this book might contribute to changing that by helping to ensure that the Nile's programs, ones such as No Child Will Drown in Our Town™, remain adequately funded. Not long ago, the club entered bankruptcy three separate times and nearly became lost. That is unacceptable. The Nile Swim Club's history is vital, as is its continued existence, as the members of its community firmly attest.

The Nile Swim Club's history is powerful. Constructed in response to rejection and hate, the club opened its doors in 1959, the first Black swim club in the United States, welcoming everybody, regardless of race, religion or ethnicity. The pool became a tool of empowerment; in the words of one member, it enabled a "level playing field." It offered the chance for thousands of Black people in Yeadon and throughout the Philadelphia region to learn how to swim, largely an opportunity afforded only to Whites. The Nile came into existence because the Yeadon Swim Club, and others like it throughout the country, refused to integrate, using the designation "private" to uphold a racist status quo.

The Nile's power transcended its pool. The club symbolized freedom. It became a cultural hub and a center of community. Nile president Anthony Patterson Sr. exudes pride in the club's past and in its present. He is the

Right: *From left*: Philadelphia chapter of Tuskegee Airmen director Mel Payne, history professor Robert J. Kodosky and Nile Swim Club president Anthony Patterson Sr. *Author's collection.*

Below: Nile Swim Club lifeguard Gabe Johnson and a young assistant. *Jacqueline Pochadt, Nile Swim Club of Yeadon Collection.*

youngest of nineteen children. Patterson's father, a pastor, died early. This left Patterson's mom to raise alone the fourteen children who remained at home. She did so admirably, returning to school, taking a job that enabled her to make ends meet and remain present for her children. This transpired a few blocks away from the Swim Club. Although Anthony's family could not afford to join, the Nile community warmly welcomed them inside. Patterson remains grateful, demonstrably committed to give back to the Nile's community all that it offered to him. It's a safe and welcoming space, one that offers Black children positive role models who look like them.

During another visit to the club, I met with many of the Nile's board members, each one proud of the Nile's past and committed to ensuring its future. Many of them are children, or grandchildren, of those who built the club. That group included predominantly Black professionals but also contained postal workers, mechanics and other blue-collar workers. Together they built one of the nation's first African American suburban communities in the West End of Yeadon, Pennsylvania. They began moving to Yeadon in the 1930s, some after coming to nearby Philadelphia as part of the early twentieth century's Great Migration of southern Black people to the North. Physicians, lawyers and businesspeople—a remarkable collection of individuals that created Philadelphia's "Black Main Line," as observers identified West Yeadon. Their professional success reflected their extraordinary perseverance, a trait that they passed on to their children. As one told me, "In our house, the mantra was, 'if there is a brick wall, go through it.'"

Such stories rendered evident to me the connection between the Nile Swim Club and the notion of securing a "Double Victory" that Black World War II veterans strove to achieve. Many of the Nile's original members and its founders served in the Second World War. After the war, one in which the U.S. military often officially prohibited them from engaging in combat operations, they refused to take no for an answer any longer. They felt no need to prove themselves to anybody. They knew that they stood capable of accomplishing whatever they wanted, and for most, that meant providing their children with opportunities that others denied them due to their skin color. If no swim club would admit them, then they would just build their own. And they did so in spectacular fashion, making sure that their children would not stand on the outside of any fence looking in.

This work tells the story of the Nile Swim Club It chronicles the club's proud history, one that includes its inspirational founding and its time in the national spotlight through its decline. Throughout, it features the

Tuskegee Airmen. *Library of Congress.*

community's extraordinary commitment to the club, demonstrated by the Nile's leadership and its members. In doing this, this work relies heavily on the words of the ones who built and preserved the club and its community. The club's leadership and its members participated in a series of oral history discussions, and these drive the narrative.

Newspaper accounts about Yeadon and the Nile supplement the story. Many of these come from the *Philadelphia Tribune*, the oldest Black newspaper in America. Billed as the "Voice of the Black community in Philadelphia," the *Tribune* is dedicated to the social, political and economic advancement of Philadelphia-area African Americans. It extensively covered the Nile in its early days. Others originate from the *Philadelphia Inquirer*, the *Philadelphia Daily News* and another Black paper, the *Philadelphia Independent*. In the 1960s, both *Ebony* and *Jet*, national Black magazines, also published stories about the Nile and Philadelphia's Black Main Line. To contextualize the Nile's story within the history of race and swimming in America, this book draws from the few existing secondary accounts, most notably Jeff Wiltse's pathbreaking *Contested Waters: A Social History of Swimming Pools* in America (University of North Carolina, 2007).

Many of the individuals who spent their childhoods at the Nile went on to become successful in a wide variety of endeavors. When asked about this, Lamont Ferrell, a producer and screenwriter, attributes this to Yeadon's Nile community. As a child, he and his friends saw their neighbors, professionals, around the neighborhood and at the club. He remembers that they freely offered guidance and mentorship. And, Ferrell says, "They looked like us." That sent a strong message. It told Ferrell and his peers as kids that "we can be whatever we want." In Ferrell's words, "We all drank that water." And it flowed from the Nile Swim Club. The story of its origin, its preservation and its ongoing success continues to inspire.

COMMUNITY OASIS

We Were Swimmers!

The Nile Swim Club's water runs deep. Formed as an oasis, it forged a community, inclusive from its onset. Its members continue to instruct and inspire, furthering the legacy of America's first Black owned and operated swim club. When it officially opened on July 11, 1959, the Nile Club welcomed more than one thousand people to its pool. There was only one problem, remembers Bill Mellix Jr., then thirteen: "None of us knew how to swim." That included Joseph William Harris, who also attended as a child. He recalls, "I had no clue how to swim." A community awaited to teach them. In his case, Harris credits Barry Williams, an older neighbor of his, for "taking me step by step. He taught me how to swim."

The Nile Swim Club remains at its original location, in Yeadon, Delaware County, Pennsylvania, immediately adjacent to Philadelphia, less than ten miles from city hall. Over the years, it became more than just a pool to the many who visited it from throughout the Greater Philadelphia area. The Nile staged community events, recreational leagues and lavish parties. It was common to spot celebrities such as Johnny Mathis, Harry Belafonte, the Supremes, D.J. Cash Money and Will Smith at the club's functions. The reason for the Nile's existence, however, remains at the core of its mission today. It teaches kids how to swim. The club's initiative, No Child Will Drown in Our Town™, rolls with conviction from the mouth of Anthony Patterson Sr., who became Nile Swim Club president in 2019.

The mission is a vital one, particularly for African American children, who continue to drown yearly at a rate consistently higher than their White peers. This situation, rooted in systemic racism, has changed little nationally since the club's creation. At that time, many of the men who frequented the pool knew how to swim. This resulted from their military training during the Second World War. Most of the women, the children's moms who spent time at the pool, had no experience in the water. They could not swim. This compelled them to ensure that their children, especially their girls, could.

Trachanda Garcia, a West Philadelphia native, remembers learning how to swim as a child at her mother's insistence. Denied the opportunity to learn how to swim as a child, Trachanda's mom made sure that her daughter received the chance. For many of the women who went to the Nile, finally as adults, their time had arrived. For all the benefits in learning how to swim, the act additionally became a symbolic gesture of freedom and equality. It proved empowering.

Lisa Ivery notes that she knew how to swim prior to her mother learning at the Nile: "My mom's big issue was that she couldn't really float; that was a fear." Ivery adds, "And she was really tall at 5' 11", but still, standing in four feet of water made her insecure. But she took the swim lessons at the Nile, and maybe she wasn't the best swimmer, but she learned how to swim."

Karen Hall Eskridge, a child of original Nile Swim Club members, recalls, "My mom didn't know how to swim, and many of the moms didn't know how to swim. And so, they all took adult swim lessons at the club, and I can remember that my mom had a real fear initially. But she got in there and got across that pool, and that was a true accomplishment for her. It was the same for the other moms." As for their daughters, Hall Eskridge says, "When we were growing up, the girls who swam were swimmers."

She stresses, "Like we were swimmers. We weren't like, 'Go put on the two-piece bathing suit and sit on the side.' We were in the water, competitive, going at it head to head." Their moms, and their dads, watched with pride. In Hall Eskridge's case, this also included diving. The *Philadelphia Tribune* reported on August 18, 1970, that on the Nile Club's Family Day, as a teenager, Hall Eskridge won the diving board competition for those thirteen years of age and over.

That family day, like others held at the Nile, featured something for everybody. The *Tribune* observed, "Beautiful people enjoyed a day of picnicking, swimming, a fashion show, hat show and dancing by the Ishangi Dancers. Fun, and plenty of it, was available the entire day." This came courtesy of the Charles E. Gordan Consistory No. 65, located in Chester,

Pennsylvania. It provided scholarship help to "promising and deserving students," along with offering support to the Shriners Children's Home.

The day it sponsored at the Nile included the "fabulous fashions and pretty young ladies" of the Tanya Madare charm school. It additionally offered the Ishangi African Dancers, directed by Ishangi Razak, who traced his roots back to Nigeria. The ensemble's performance, the *Tribune* noted, proved "highly informative" and utilized African instruments and "costumes that were colorful and handmade." At the Nile, however, the swimming pool always remains at the center of it all, and that day proved no different; several swimming competitions were staged in addition to those held for diving. As Swim Club vice-president Lisa Ivery observes, "Swimming should not be a luxury for only some."

This notion remained uncommon, however, as the young Nile swimmers learned when they left the club. Current Nile Swim Club president Anthony Patterson Sr. remembers a time at the Nile's pool as a child: "I learned the way folks did when you jumped into eleven feet of water. They watched me, taught me how to doggie paddle and then swim. I just got pretty good at it." Then he remembers, "They taught me how to dive and showed me how to do one and a halves, back flips, all that stuff." After graduating from high school, Patterson went to Cheyney University, an HBCU. He remembers, "When I went to Cheyney and the pool was open, they were very pleasantly surprised to learn that I could swim and dive. A lot of folks at Cheyney University could not go into the deep end of the water."

A similar scenario transpired when Mark Miller, a son of one of the original members, arrived at Penn State University and took the required swim test. "Every freshman there then," Miller explains, "had to take a swim test. If you couldn't pass it, you had to take a swimming class." He says, "I went with my friends who were predominantly White. I jumped into the pool. We had to tread water for two minutes or something like that." He remembers, "We were swimming around and telling the lifeguards, 'Hey, it looks like this person isn't going to make it, bring the hook!'" He laughs, "And here I am swimming around these White guys who can't. I said, 'I can swim, but I can't float, because Black people can't float!'" He says, "That was a real revelation about how unique my experience was, learning how to swim and becoming a fairly strong swimmer."

For others, the revelation of the unique opportunity that the Nile presented to its young swimmers occurred before college. As a child when visiting her cousins down south, Hall Eskridge learned that none of them could swim. There existed no facilities and no lessons—only rivers and streams. So that is

Nile Swim Club president Anthony Patterson Sr. keeping watch at the pool. *Jacqueline Pochadt, Nile Swim Club of Yeadon Collection.*

where Hall Eskridge took her cousins, intent on teaching them how to swim. As she says, "I knew how to swim and taught them. And we would swim in the river; for them, that was a big deal. They didn't have pools." It nearly became a bigger deal. Hall Eskridge acquired her skills at the Nile, which possessed none of the natural characteristics of its namesake, or, for that matter, of any other natural body of water.

Still, Hall Eskridge possessed a great deal of confidence. She recalls, "One time we were in the river, and I'm like, I'm going to show them how to do this. So, I'm swimming, swimming, swimming." All her cousins started to pull back. Hall Eskridge yelled, "What's the matter? Y'all chickens." Her cousins responded, "The snakes are over there." Hall Eskridge laughs, "I learned that day something about swimming in the wild you gotta understand."

The Environment Is Just Better

When the Nile Swim Club opened its doors in 1959, it enabled Black folks in Yeadon a unique opportunity. No other such space existed nationally. Swim clubs exemplified White privilege. While Black people, in the North anyway, had access to urban public pools, they offered no instruction and little chance to swim. In his article "Swimming Pools as Contested Places," Jeff Wiltse, a professor of history at the University of Montana and the author of the award-winning *Contested Waters: A Social History of Pools in America*, observed that by the middle of the 1960s, "Public officials briefly prioritized the recreational needs of Black Americans."

The federal government funded the construction of hundreds of urban public pools. Wiltse labeled these "mini pools," as they measured twenty by forty feet, with a uniform water depth of three feet. According to Wiltse, these "mini pools" failed to provide "viable recreation or encourage actual swimming." Enclosed by chain link fences, the "mini pools," with narrow concrete perimeters, lacked changing rooms or any other type of amenity. Shortly after the Nile opened, George F. Brown, writing for *Jet* magazine, observed, "In many northern cities—and some southern cities—Negroes are free to swim in public pools. But a vast number of them don't like to swim in public pools, which are often so glutted with humanity that swimming is merely a term and not an actuality." Besides, Brown suggested, "The conduct of many elements in public pools repels more reserved persons."

As Wiltse chronicled, the history of racially integrated swimming pools in the United States is complex. Northern cities built the nation's first public pools during the late nineteenth century to enable poor working-class boys, both Black and White, to bathe. In early twentieth-century Pittsburgh, as Wiltse explained in "Swimming Against Segregation: The Struggle to Desegregate," in gender-segregated pools built to "promote cleanliness and physical health among the city's working classes," no issues existed between the "blacks and Whites despite their close intermingling at the pools."

That changed, in Pittsburgh and elsewhere, as pools became recreational destinations in the 1930s and permitted males and females to swim together. Wiltse noted, "White swimmers suddenly objected to the presence of blacks and quite literally beat them out of the water." This resulted from the sudden intersection of race and gender. As Wiltse observed, "Whites did not want black men interacting with White women at such an intimate public space."

By law or by force, public pools became racially segregated spaces. When the U.S. Supreme Court ruled in 1954 that racial segregation in education violated the Constitution, activists began demanding the desegregation of other public spaces, including swimming pools. As a result, like in Yeadon, Whites abandoned public pools to create private swim clubs. This enabled them to let in, and to keep out, whomever they chose. And despite the

Supreme Court's decision and the activism it inspired, public swimming spaces remained contested.

In their article "Our Color Won't Wash Off: The Desegregation of Swimming in Lancaster, Pennsylvania," historians M. Alison Kibler and Shanni Davidowitz shared the experience of Lancaster resident Louis Butcher Jr. He told them of his visit to Rocky Springs Amusement Park as a child with his mother. When his mom "bought tickets for him to use the park's facilities, the attendant explained to her that the pool was off limits for African Americans." Butcher added, "So we left."

Segregated pools denied Black people the chance to learn how to swim under the supervision of lifeguards. Many chose to avoid water, but others took to natural bodies of water, unsupervised and unschooled in swimming. The founders of the Nile Swim Club sought to remedy this, without malice, in 1959. Decades later, their mission remains necessary. Jeff Wiltse identified several "racially charged confrontations" that transpired at swimming pools during the summer of 2018. He observed that "the common thread" running through them all constituted "a White person's assumption [that] Black people do not belong at swimming pools, at least not the same pools that Whites use."

Learning to swim, with lifeguard Nellda Harris, is not a luxury. *Jacqueline Pochadt, Nile Swim Club of Yeadon Collection.*

This certainly helps explain why, according to the Centers for Disease Control and Prevention (CDC), between 1999 and 2019, the drowning rate of Blacks exceeded that of Whites by 1.5 times. The CDC asserts that "the disparity in rates among Black persons compared with White persons increased significantly from 2005–2019. Drowning death rates are associated with persistent and concerning racial/ethnic disparities." City pools that serve predominantly Black populations generally pale in comparison to the Nile. "So, as one who has run those city pools," says Nile aquatic director Nita Dunham, "it is just a difference. The environment is calmer at the Nile. The people who are there really want to be there. The environment is just better."

The Nile Kept Me Out of Tough Times

According to Nile Swim Club lifeguard Josie Jones, "At the beginning of the summer at the Nile, there is a lot of splashing, especially the young people [who] are nervous." But, she says, "being at the Nile, the safety is there. It has all the training, free classes that range from babies to adults. That is rare." Jones explains, "The city pools may not have enough resources to offer adult swim. They just don't have the resources that we have at the Nile." Dunham adds that free lessons offered by the city pools "are not as frequent" as ones provided by the Nile. Moreover, "We have a great teaching staff at the Nile. The ratios are pretty good with the number of instructors that we have." Dunham further notes "the high level of training for instructors at the Nile. It is different in the city, where sometimes the lifeguards teach, but they haven't received any teacher training."

The Nile Swim Club's historical significance is apparent. So, too, is its continued importance, and not just for the top-notch swimming instruction it freely provides. Karen Hall Eskridge affirms that the club is "probably even more important in 2023 than it was in 1959." Back then, the "pool opened because we knew we weren't wanted in certain spaces." But, as she suggests, the more things change, the more they remain the same. "In 2023, it's about not having to assimilate into a space where you are not really welcome" and "being very comfortable in a space that you've developed and grown, and that reflects you."

Hall Eskridge believes that "now it's even more important that our kids see that. Nobody wants to be in an environment where your actions can be misinterpreted solely because of the color of your skin." She cites the Nile's significance as a place where one can go and "not have that judgement, and not have that feeling just hanging over your head. Our kids need that; our adults need that. It's a safe place where everybody can enjoy themselves, be themselves, among people that look like them."

In discussing whether society has progressed since the Nile Swim Club opened, Hall Eskridge thoughtfully suggests, "I think it depends on how you look at progress." About the club's continued capacity to provide Black swimmers with a safe space, Hall Eskridge says, "If that is not perceived from the outside as being progress, it is because its Black folks owning something that they are very comfortable with, take pride in, and don't feel the need to assimilate. If that is not being viewed as progressive, is 'progressive' only when it includes White folks?"

Nile Swim Club lifeguard Josie Jones says without hesitation, "The Nile is progressive." She explains, "It brings families, people of all ages and generations. There is something for everybody at the Nile. If you're a swimmer, that is great. If not, there are people there to teach you." As a preschool teacher, Jones is especially fond of the club's "Water Babies" initiative, which teaches toddlers to swim. Besides, she adds, "There is always something new. Every year you see growth," from the addition of tennis courts to the community garden. Jones says, "Healthy eating is everything. It is what we need for our children to thrive in this time." She adds, "And being African American swimmers from the inner city is something that is rare. Its kept me out of a lot of tough times."

My Parents Had a Process

According to one of the Nile's founders, Carson Puriefoy, the Swim Club resulted from a collective resolve not to let their "Black children looking over the fence of the White pool wondering if they could get in." In the 1950s, racial integration in Yeadon ended with the last bell of the school day. Church Lane served as the unofficial divide between Black West Yeadon and the rest of the borough populated by Whites. Lauretta Miller moved into West Yeadon with her family in 1959. She clearly remembers her realtor advising that "Negroes will never cross Church Lane." At that time, Jacquelynn Puriefoy notes, as an African American, "You couldn't even go to the stores on Church Lane."

Bill Mellix Jr. graduated from Yeadon High School in 1964. The class totaled 104 students, with about 20 of them Black. The school occupied the intersection of Bailey Road and Cypress Road. Mellix Jr. recalls, "If you drove by that school when I was there, all the Black kids came out of the door on Bailey Road, and all the White kids went out the door on Cypress Road. That wasn't because of segregation—that's just the way everybody left to get to their homes. It was just closest to where you were going."

In school, Mellix Jr. notes, "We all got along; there wasn't a lot of outward racism in school." West Yeadon covered six blocks, and its residents represented an emergent Black professional class that included doctors, lawyers and teachers. Mellix Jr.'s dad worked at the U.S. Post Office and additionally ran a small landscaping company. Parents in West Yeadon expected the children to attend college, and many did, gaining acceptance into top schools such as the University of Pennsylvania and Drexel University. Mellix Jr.'s classmates included Paula Dow, New Jersey's first Black woman attorney general; artist Lorene Corey; and Ross Love, the first African American vice-president for Proctor & Gamble.

At Yeadon High, however, Mellix Jr. remembers that the guidance counselor "only gave us catalogues to Cheyney, Lincoln and Howard University," all HBCUs. Mellix Jr. played on the school's football team and "really believed I should be the quarterback my senior year." He instead played defensive back and wide receiver. "They didn't want a Black quarterback," Mellix Jr. states. "Back then they said the quarterbacks had to be intelligent." Norman Miller says that for the students, the integrated Yeadon High served as a "neutral ground." That did not prevent Bill Mellix Jr. from getting locked up on graduation night. He remembers, "The cops took Gary Toombs home; they thought he was White. They took me to jail."

When Wendy D. Puriefoy attended Yeadon High School in the 1960s, according to her sister Jacquelynn, the school's counselors "were suggesting that she go to a vocational school." This did not sit well with Nile Swim Club founder Carson Puriefoy and his wife, Betty. "Of course," Jacquelynn states, "my parents wouldn't hear that." Wendy went on to receive her BA from William Smith College in New York, where she became the first student trustee elected to sit on the board of trustees.

After taking her undergraduate degree in 1971, a year later she completed an MA in history at Boston University. In 2007, Hobart and William Smith Colleges awarded her the President's Medal for her "passionate and effective" work as an "advocate for education equity for disadvantaged children." Jackie notes with satisfaction, "My mother, when the newspaper appeared, she marched up to the high school and made them get a glass thing to put the clippings in there." She adds, "Wendy is brilliant, I mean really brilliant."

Jacquelynn's time at Yeadon High proved even more tumultuous than her sister's. She "got in a lot of trouble" there because "she spoke out." She knew that her parents had her back. "That's what they wanted us to do; they didn't want us to take a back seat." In one instance, Jacquelynn remembers her history teacher, "and it was in the history book," instructing that "Black people have big hearts and small brains." Jacquelynn stood up and said, "That's a lie." This resulted in a heated debate. "We really got into it," Jacquelynn recalls, "and, of course, I was suspended." She continues, "I wasn't going to take that. And it was always something. I'll never forget the algebra teacher. I spent a large part of my life hoping something terrible would happen to her," Jacquelynn laughs, "and that I could be there to see it. She was awful, awful to us." Others acted the same.

Rai Nelson, originally from South Philadelphia, moved to Yeadon with her husband when they married in 1965. She worked for the Social Security Administration, while her husband first served as a police officer in nearby Darby and then went to work at a corrections facility as a social worker. When asked what it was like in Yeadon having a kid, Rai responds, "That's a loaded question." She explains, "It was very nice having a kid in Yeadon. It was a nice area, but it wasn't always easy to have a Black child in Yeadon. That's where the difficulties came in." Rai specifies that these resulted from the family's decision for their daughter, Lisa, to attend the local parochial school, St. Louis. The school no longer exists, but Rai says that for Lisa, "It was very difficult then; she was discriminated against."

Lisa began her education in the public school. While there, she received support for her dyslexia, diagnosed while in kindergarten. Lisa recalls, "Every day, I would be taken out of class and worked with, along with other students, for my dyslexia. It was just amazing, looking back on it now. That was a blessing." She credits the help she received for never feeling "like it prohibited me going forward with any real challenges." Despite the positive experience, Lisa's paternal grandmother proved "adamant" that Lisa transfer to St. Louis, "of the mindset that we [would] get a better education."

Lisa recalls the mantra, "We're not sending you to school to make friends; we're sending you to get an education." Lisa explains, "With parents coming of age in the civil rights movement, I think having access to that type of education was important to them. And my grandmother, being very active civically, being able to provide that sort of access was very important to her."

For Lisa, her new school delivered regarding the educational resources. The issues stemmed from the reality that, as she says, "I was the only one [Black student]." Her mother, Rai, adds, "And that was the time of *Roots*," the televised miniseries derived from Alex Haley's 1976 novel that traces the lives of the author's ancestors back to American slavery. Widely watched, the program aired on seven consecutive nights in January 1977. This led, Rai remembers, to people at Lisa's school calling her "Kizzy," the only member of the family depicted in *Roots* to spend her entire life as a slave. Perplexed, Lisa asked her mom why they called her this name and why the school's crossing guard routinely said, "You can cross the street now, Kizzy." That prompted a nun, cites Rai, "to write me, I can almost quote her: 'I would thank you to tell your daughter not to bring her problems home to you.'"

Lisa says, "I remember it quite clearly; I was in the sixth grade." Lisa found herself ostracized and isolated. Rai notes that her peers would "have parties at their house that she was not invited to because she was Black." Lisa applauds her mother for "keeping me very active so that I didn't notice. I was like, 'I can't go anyway because I have dance class,' or whatever it was. My mom made sure I was otherwise engaged so that I didn't feel left out." When asked if the school employed any Black administrators or faculty, Lisa responds, "Not even the janitor."

Lisa believes that the experience, and the way her parents handled it, enabled her to develop a strong sense of self-reliance. She says, "My parents had a process, without even realizing they had a process. We would talk about my day, and if I brought up something, they would talk me through a strategy." Lisa states with pride, "My parents taught me self-advocacy and agency; it was very empowering."

Community for Life

For Karen Hall Eskridge and her peers, the children of West Yeadon in the 1960s, "Those formative years, between thirteen and fifteen, when you can go left or right, the Nile offered a great environment for keeping you centered, on track and balanced." Hall Eskridge singles out the lifeguards as "so important." She recalls, "They would sit down and talk to you. Talk to you about college, about jobs. I mean they would talk to you about anything that you had an interest of talking about."

Maintenance worker Shae Thomas with Nile Swim Club board treasurer Deborah Barnes. *Cheri Carter.*

Hall Eskridge, one of six children, whose parents did not attend college, found the chance to talk to those who did attend to be insightful. She says, "Like, neither of my parents went to college, so they couldn't talk to us about college experience or even how you went about considering a college. So, we had this coming in, people who were living it and could educate you about these things." And, as Hall Eskridge adds, they "were both genders, male and female."

Many of the lifeguards who worked at the pool during the 1960s came from Philadelphia, where they worked as teachers. According to Hall Eskridge, they provided exemplary role models for her and others who worked at the pool. She explains that when there, "this work ethic they had was ingrained in you. Being an employee, it didn't matter that your parents were founding members or whatever. You were an employee. You had your jobs, did them and got paid accordingly. The work ethic was a really big thing."

But as Hall Eskridge stresses, the mentoring did not end when the pool closed. "But then it was just a really, strong network, one that remains in place today, of contacts and people. Even though it was only three months out of the year, it's not like these people were in your life [and] then out of your life. We never thought about it back then, but we received great mentoring in that environment." The Nile Swim Club generated a pride among its members that proved uplifting for members throughout their lives.

A BLACK SUBURBAN ENCLAVE

Yeadon Jim Crow

For kids growing up in West Yeadon, it proved crucial to have strong mentors in their community, ones who looked like them and who frequented the Swim Club. Otherwise, they rarely if ever encountered teachers who looked like them in the schools they attended. The Educational Equality League of Philadelphia brought this to the attention of the State of Pennsylvania in November 1961. It additionally questioned the treatment of students at the predominantly Black Evans Elementary School. On November 18, 1961, the *Philadelphia Tribune* reported, "The State Human Relations Commission is looking into complaints of racial discrimination against the Yeadon School Board."

These allegations included "charges that Negro pupils are forced to use an old church building" to "relieve overcrowded conditions at the almost all-Negro Evans Elementary School." This despite that "the virtually all-White Bell Avenue School has an under-enrollment." The second complaint alleged that "the Yeadon school board rejected the applications of three qualified Negro teachers for employment." Underrepresentation of Black faculty characterized Yeadon High's teaching staff until it merged with nearby Lansdowne and Darby to create Penn Wood High School in the early 1980s.

The *Tribune* noted in its 1961 story that it learned "the State Fair Practice Commission requested the names of the teachers that the Yeadon board allegedly sidetracked." These included two Yeadon residents: Jacqualin B. Mosley, who resided at 123 East Providence Road, and Christine T. Wilson, who lived at 3 Robin Road. Floyd L. Logan, president of the Educational Equality League (EEL), who filed the charges, found the news of the investigation "very heartening." He clarified that Yeadon did not qualify as an exception, arguing that "the racial situation" in schools throughout Pennsylvania "should be adjusted."

In the article, the *Tribune* observed that "Yeadon is rated as one of the most exclusive Negro living areas in the Delaware Valley. Most of its residents are top bracket business and professional men and women, including many teachers." It then added, "All but a few Negroes, however, live in the section of Yeadon known as the West End." A year later, on December 22, 1962, the *Philadelphia Tribune* informed its readers that "the Pennsylvania Human Relations Commission told the Yeadon School Board Monday night that it has found no evidence that the board has discriminated against Negro applicants for teaching jobs." Immediately, Floyd L. Logan expressed his "disappointment." He criticized the decision in a letter he wrote to Dr. Charles H. Boehm, superintendent, Department of Public Instruction, located in the state capital of Harrisburg, Pennsylvania.

Logan found the dismissal "inconceivable" and "was also disturbed" by Boehm's "lack of cooperation" in providing the Educational Equality League with the results of the investigation. A press release from Boehm's office claimed that "it would be impractical to transfer students from the Bell School to the Evans." It further cited that "Colored applicants had been interviewed for teaching positions, but no qualified applicant had been found to recommend to the Yeadon School Board."

In a follow-up to the investigation, the Pennsylvania Human Relations Commission (PHRC) expressed hope that "the Yeadon School District will consider applications from minority group persons on an equal basis with other applicants and that selections be made without regard to race, color, religious creed or national origin." About that statement, on December 22, 1962, in the article "One No Did Not Stop Yeadon Jim Crow," the *Philadelphia Tribune* asked, "How ridiculous can the Commission get?"

The *Tribune* observed, "In one breath it states that there is no evidence of discrimination and in the next it hopes the Board will consider applications on an equal basis." The *Tribune* also pointed out that "the record shows that not one Negro teacher is employed in the Yeadon School District," despite that "many Philadelphia Negro teachers live in Yeadon." It continued further noted that "several Negro applicants have filed to teach there during the years; that records have been destroyed."

In addition to criticizing the PHRC's decision, the *Tribune* faulted the commission for being "very careful to point out that Rev. William H. Gray, a Negro, a guidance specialist in the State Department of Public Instruction, investigated the charges and found no evidence of discrimination." It accused the commission of attempting to "give a positive assurance that since a Negro investigator stated that he found no discrimination, of course, there was none." The paper suggested this was problematic. It offered that "without any reflection on Dr. Gray, that there are all kinds of Negroes just like there are all kinds of Whites. They are not all the same any more than are all White."

Educational Equality League president Floyd L. Logan echoed the *Tribune*'s dissatisfaction with the decision in a letter sent to Pennsylvania's governor-elect, William W. Scranton. He cited the commission's lack of transparency and felt "disturbed by the lack of cooperation from Dr. Boehm with furnishing the League with the results of his investigation."

Soon after, in February 1962, the *Philadelphia Tribune* reported that "another organization has trained its guns on the alleged racial discrimination practiced by the Yeadon Borough School Board." In a "stand similar to that advanced six weeks ago by the Educational Equality League," the *Tribune* observed, "the Darby Branch NAACP [National Association for the Advancement of Colored People]…protest the racially discriminatory hiring policies of the Public School Boards of the eastern section of Delaware County, especially in the Yeadon Borough."

The NAACP asserted that "qualified Negro applicants for teaching positions in this borough meet the 'blank wall of racial discrimination' and therefore are denied available positions." Gladys J. Roye, NAACP president, stated that her organization "received numerous complaints from parents and teacher applicants concerning the racial policies of the Yeadon School System."

Yeadon High

Born in 1944, Yvonne Burnley Studevan attended Yeadon High at the time of its investigation. One of twelve Black students in the school, she recalls that "most of us started out together in kindergarten and went all the way through to the twelfth grade. There might have been a few that came in along the way." She says, "Being Black in Yeadon, I knew there were certain things I could and could not do. For example, in high school, Black girls could not be cheerleaders, but we could carry the flag. We could be flag girls, but we couldn't be majorettes. Some of those things bothered me." Still, Burnley Studevan cites that she did "play a lot of sports" and "got a good education."

By the time Karen Hall Eskridge attended Yeadon High School later in the 1960s, Yeadon High School employed a few Black faculty. This resulted in more controversy. Hall Eskridge remembers, "With my age group, it was the beginning of the Black Panthers, Nikki Giovanni was all the rage and we were coming into Black Power. We were pretty vocal." Hall Eskridge remembers as a child watching the events of the civil rights movement transpire on television with her mother.

None of this sat well with some of the older faculty, including the history teacher (still there) who had made the comment to Jacquelynn Puriefoy-Brinkley's class about Black people having large hearts and small brains. "My class," according to Hall Eskridge, "we had a good deal of smart people. We were very opinionated, and some of it was controversial." Hall Eskridge remembers, for instance, that "one of our first Black teachers played the Last Poets in class." Recognized by music critics as one of the earliest influences on hip hop music, the Last Poets sprang from the civil rights movement's Black nationalism.

Originally a trio comprising Abiodun Owewole, Gylan Kain and David Nelson, they derived their group's name from South African poet Keoranpetse Kgositsile's declaration that guns would soon replace poetry. Classic poems from the Last Poets include "This Is Madness" and "When the Revolution Comes." As one might imagine, Hall Eskridge recalls, "This caused a big brouhaha. But she was very aware and wanted us, as Black students, to be aware. Of course, they wanted to fire her, for her to quit. But our parents stood behind her. I think we were coming into our own at that point."

Kenneth Earl Green graduated from Yeadon High School in 1971. He says, "Our class was maybe 25 percent Black." He remembers that at that time, a growing awareness of Black history "was getting started." As a result, in school he and his Black classmates "put on skits" to dramatize historical personalities and events. According to Green, this prompted "a couple of our White classmates to walk out." He says that he and other Black students went to the principal and told him, "If we had done that we would have been suspended." Years later at a reunion, Green spoke with a former White classmate. He told her, "You know, we thought we were on par with you all." She responded by telling him, "No, you all were above us."

Denise Stewart Swann, a student at Yeadon High at about the same time as Hall Eskridge and Green, recalls, "It wasn't very equal, I must say." She says, "There was definitely some prejudice going on, but it wasn't everybody." Stewart Swann had White friends and even, at times, as a cheerleader, went "over to the house of one of the other girls who lived closer to school and change clothes." She additionally recalls her friends Boni and Merle inviting her to their Bas Mitzvahs. She attended both. But, Stewart Swann adds, "we were blind to our limits." For example, according to Stewart Swann, "They had usually had limits on things. I was a cheerleader, but one of two—that is all they would allow when I was in seventh grade." She additionally ran into a barrier when attempting to don the school mascot's uniform. "Many were not in favor of that. But somehow, between my mother and my brother, who had relationships with some of the cheerleaders, in kindergarten I was the cheerleader mascot when he played football."

After she graduated from Yeadon, Stewart Swann, daughter of Nile Swim Club founder Elmer William Stewart, attended Cheyney University, a local historically Black college with an outstanding reputation for teacher training. While there, Stewart Swann did a portion of her student teaching at her alma mater, and that led to a full-time position. Stewart Swann became a math teacher at Yeadon High School in 1976. She went on to teach for forty-one years, twenty-eight of those in Yeadon and Lansdowne. A remarkable accomplishment, considering that as late as 2021 72 percent of math teachers are White, according to Zippia, while only 8 percent are Black.

According to Nicole M. Joseph's study, "The Invisibility of Black Girls in Mathmatics," this dearth of Black women teaching math derives from "Teachers' low expectations and overall assumptions about Black girls in society." A pioneer educator, Stewart Swann found herself nearly isolated from colleagues who shared her skin color, in any discipline, teaching at Yeadon. "We used to tease," she says, "that Yeadon would only allow three Blacks in as teachers. And all three of us were from Cheyney."

In an interview, Stewart Swann says, "Let me just tell you one quick thing about the social studies teacher. He was the only Black male teacher in the building. One time he was in my classroom after school. He came in and was teasing me about something. And I also had a student in my classroom. When my colleague left, the student said to me, 'Are you going

Left to right: Denise Stewart Swann, Louise Weley Stewart, Ronald L. Swann, Danielle Stewart Magee and William A. Stewart. *Jacqueline Pochadt, Nile Swim Club of Yeadon Collection.*

to let a janitor talk to you like that?' And, of course, that is because the only Black males that the student saw in the building were janitors. He didn't realize a Black man might be a teacher."

At that time, the student population at Yeadon High remained predominantly White. This, at times, put Stewart Swann in precarious positions. She remembers, "I would face some difficulties once in a while." She cites one class she encountered her first year. At the time, it caused her to reflect, "If I can make it through this, I can make it through anything." In that class, one then considered as low achieving, Stewart Swann recalls, "I had some students, one in particular. He had carved into his arm 'KKK Kill [racist epithet].' That is some of what I had to deal with."

A student at Yeadon High in the 1970s, Wanda Reese remembers student life as relatively tranquil. She says, "Around tenth grade, there was the first interracial couple dating. That was a big deal, but after about ten minutes, everybody said 'whatever' and moved on." Boundaries outside of school, however, remained firm. Now living on the other side of Yeadon, "where we weren't allowed to live, back in the day," Reese says, White friends who lived there might say to her, "We're friends and all, but you can't come to my house because my parents wouldn't allow it." Otherwise,

The family of founder Elmer and Florence Stewart. *First row*: Caitlyn Fassnacht, Louise Wesley Stewart, Noelle Stewart Fassnacht, Victoria Fassnacht, Dylan Hubert and Dominique Byars Hubert. *Second row*: James Fassnacht, William (Bill) Stewart, Ronald Swann, Denise Stewart Swann and Bilal Hubert.

she remembers, "We all got along. I can't remember any fighting. If there was, it was over something dumb."

At times, however, student attitudes remained at odd with those of adults. Lamont Ferrell, a basketball star at Yeadon who earned a scholarship to play at Temple University, recalls "a young lady who was a cheerleader in high school that I was interested in. And she happened to be White." He says, "I found out she was interested in me, and we became really close friends. We started to sort of date." This did not go unnoticed. Ferrell remembers that "the coaches pulled me into their office." They said, "We see you and your friend are getting a little close and, you know, there's a lot of people out there that might not like that." Ferrell stood shocked. He says, "I was like, wow man, this is crazy. It's like 1920. You can't just walk a girl home?"

In the early 1980s, Yeadon High School ceased to exist. Lansdowne, Darby and Yeadon consolidated to create Penn Wood High School. Lisa

Ivery graduated from Penn Wood in 1986. She says, "I think our energy was different." She remembers friend groups as mixed racially, while no restrictions, or safety concerns, existed in visiting other parts of Yeadon and Lansdowne. Elsewhere proved different. Ivery recalls, "I would say there were a lot of towns around us that I wasn't going to hang out in." She cites Upper Darby, for example, as one that "was predominantly White and not so friendly." While her and her brother frequented the shops on 69th Street, they would take the bus directly there and back, not straying into adjacent neighborhoods.

Ivery remembers that for Black students, there still did "exist lines." Lisa tried out for the field hockey team, "really knowing nothing about the sport at the time," and she made the team. So did her friend, also named Lisa, another Black student. Besides the two of them, Lisa notes, there were "of course, not a lot of Blacks on the field hockey field." She mentions no ill treatment except the prohibition she encountered in wanting to join her White teammates at the racially exclusive Lansdowne Swim Club. The merger that created Penn Wood fostered better interracial relations, but Black students continued to lack teachers who looked like them. Penn Wood High's African American faculty remained a distinct minority. Ivery remembers "maybe five or six Black faculty, definitely not a balance."

Kathleen Wainwright graduated from Penn Wood High School in 1995. She says, "By then, we had a mix, but we didn't have a lot of Black teachers. But the ones that resonated with me most were the ones from the neighborhood." Wainwright remembers, "Ms. Byars (Stewart Swann), she grew up with my mom. She was our teacher in high school. Also, there was Ms. Johnson and Ms. Porter, the ones who knew my mom, the ones we grew up, the ones we saw at the Nile. I don't have a bunch of memorable teachers from back then, except the ones I knew from the neighborhood."

DOWN THE WAY

From the aggressions they confronted at school, micro and macro in scope, West Yeadon offered a haven, for both the children and their parents. There existed plenty of trees, open fields and, as Mellix Jr. recalls fondly, "the freedom to ride our bikes in the streets." Lamont Ferrell moved to Yeadon's Orchard Street, adjacent to West Yeadon. By that time, the mid-1970s, blocks on the periphery of West Yeadon had begun to integrate. Ferrell remembers that as kids, he and his friends referred to West Yeadon as "down the way" and East Yeadon as "up the way." Where he lived "was considered 'up the way,'" Ferrell says, but "a lot of our friends lived 'down the way.'" And that led him to the Nile. It "was right in viewing distance," he recalls, and for someone who went on to play basketball at Temple University, the lure of the club's court proved irresistible.

Lamont Ferrell, a screenwriter and producer, thought that when his family arrived in Yeadon, they landed in Mayberry, the town setting for the 1950s sitcom *The Andy Griffith Show*. He remembers, "My neighbor had their milk delivered. A guy would pull up in a truck and put a bottle of milk right on their stoop, in a little container. I never saw that before." For Ferrell, "It really was like the 1950s." This provided an ideal setting for the Ferrell family, one that included six children, all boys. As the middle child, Lamont grew up with two older brothers and three younger ones. While his dad worked to manage food concessions at the Philadelphia International Airport, his mom stayed at home to manage the household and family. They moved to Yeadon from West Philadelphia, living on 43rd Street. It was a short distance driving, maybe thirty minutes in time, but seemingly a world away.

The Ferrell family left West Philadelphia to escape the escalating gang violence in the city. Ferrell remembers that "a gang tried to recruit my oldest

The Ferrells: Terryl, Jacin, Dion, Stephen, LaMont, Jamar (depicted on Lamont's shirt) Willie and Willamae Ferrell, 2014. *Shawn Ferrell.*

brother Terryl into their ranks. They literally came up to the house and tried to pull him off the porch. It was a big thing," Ferrell says, "so shortly after that we moved." Ferrell recalls it vividly. "I remember driving up and seeing we had a driveway and a yard with grass." And there was more. Ferrell's uncle installed a basketball hoop as a surprise for the kids before the family arrived. "So, y'know, for a bunch of boys to come in and have their own basketball court in the backyard, grass to cut, a long driveway," Ferrell smiles at the memory, "it was amazing."

And then they saw the Nile. Ferrell says, "It was like an oasis, man. It was even more mythical than that milk—it was a Black swim club!" Even today, Ferrell notes, "not many people can access pools. Back then, if you could, it was like the Jeffersons—they must be rich!" Even then, Ferrell understood the club's significance and learned about its history. But his family did not become members; with one income and six children, they could not afford it. That did not keep them away. "We would use guest passes from our friends or maybe pay the day rate," Ferrell remembers, "And, of course, full disclosure, sometimes we would jump the fence—we always seemed to find a way in."

Once in, the Swim Club provided the oasis it promised. "You really felt safe," Ferrell recalls. "Your parents didn't have to worry about you, and all of your friends were in there." Ferrell enjoyed it all—the pool, the snack bar and, especially, the basketball court. He played there often and later returned to coach the next group of kids coming up. Ferrell says, "It was all just great. I had such a wonderful upbringing in Yeadon, and the Nile was like the icing on the cake."

The son of an original Nile Swim club member, Norman Miller Jr. reflects that "you can't paint it as a utopian place; they weren't all happy days, but we had enough good ones that others end up in the back of your head somewhere." When Miller hears people "talk about having a bad childhood," he confesses, "I can't relate to that. I had a fantastic childhood." He acknowledges, "The Nile Swim Club played a big part in that." Kenneth Green adds that growing up in West Yeadon, "We lived in a bubble." He laughs, "But maybe some of us took that for granted and didn't study as much as we should have."

Joseph William Harris describes that bubble as "an area where everybody had pride in themselves, pride in their homes; they took care of their property. It was a beautiful area." Karen Hall Eskridge stresses, "It was a nice community. No locked doors; we would just go in each other's houses," she laughs, "maybe not their refrigerators, but definitely in and out of the houses." South Philadelphia native Rai Nelson recalls seeing Yeadon for the first time and thinking of it as "God's country." She says, "If you were raised in an urban area like South Philadelphia, like I was, Yeadon with its grass and trees, well, it's a very different experience."

It provided a setting that Yvonne Burnley Studevan arranged to witness with a bird's-eye view. She recalls, "I loved to hang upside down." An oak tree stood outside of her grandmother's house, one that Burnley Studenvan remembers "being to small to jump up and reach the bottom limb. But then one day I jumped up and caught it." From that day, she "would climb that tree to the top and look out over the neighborhood to see what was going on." She adds jokingly, "I was really nosy!"

Building a Black Suburban Bubble

That experience was due to the originals, the ones who built that bubble, who created one of America's earliest suburban Black communities. They included Burnley Studevan's grandparents, who left Burlington, New Jersey, to settle in Yeadon at the onset of the Great Depression. According to a 1987 article in the *Philadelphia Inquirer* by Roy H. Campbell, "The times of Yeadon's black enclave," the construction of Yeadon's Black bubble, one of the earliest African American suburban communities in the United States, came about because of the Great Depression.

During that economic crisis, "many white businessmen lost their mortgages, and few people could afford to buy large colonial houses," like those that lined Yeadon's Fairview Avenue. As a result, after their owners abandoned these houses and vandalism began, "Blacks started to move in after a group of real estate agents put the houses up for sale or rent to anyone with the money." Campbell noted, "Many fell in love with the wooded area where pheasants and rabbits could be hunted." Word spread widely.

Yvonne Burnley Studevan says that her grandfather was "looking for a place near Philadelphia and heard that Yeadon was an up and coming area." She adds that "there were already a few Black families there." Indeed, Yeadon already had become a center for suburban Philadelphia's Black political and social activity. On March 31, 1932, for example, the *Philadelphia Tribune* reported of Yeadon's Hazel Bell creation of the Colored Women's Federation of Social and Political Clubs of Delaware County. The *Tribune* described the club as a "movement to group social and political clubs already organized into a cooperating body of women who are interested in the general advancement of colored female citizens."

The Colored Women's Federation sought to "sponsor those pioneer women laboring under adverse conditions to help raise the standard of living in our communities." Black social clubs located in Yeadon in the early 1930s included the Night Owl Club and the Pecunaris Club. These often featured dinner parties that included card playing and music. Politically, Yeadon residents founded the West End Yeadon Republican Club, which came to meet at the American Legion Hall on Bailey Road. It doubled as a social outlet. In September 1932, the *Philadelphia Tribune* reported that "The Colored Republican Club gave a dance on Labor Day." There additionally existed regular efforts by individuals to bring community members together.

In April 1933, the *Tribune* identified Miss Ophelia James of Yeadon as one who entertained guests on Easter Monday. It further observed, "Perhaps one of the outstanding events on the social calendar was the birthday party given by Mr. William Prattis of Yeadon." Held at a social club in nearby Darby, the event welcomed forty-eight guests. Once inside, according to the *Tribune*, they found that "the artistic taste of Mr. Prattis was expressed in every detail. The Spacious hall was decorated with ferns and spring flowers."

Unlike many of Yeadon's early Black residents who moved there from the city, Burnley Studevan's grandparents came from a rural existence. Back in Burlington, in the house her grandfather built, her grandparents "had a much larger house, a larger yard." In Yeadon, they lived in a twin house with no yard. This proved an adjustment that Yeadon's woods rendered possible. Burnley Studevan says, "At that time, there were a lot of wooded areas nearby; she could go pick sassafras and other things that she was accustomed to. I think she adjusted, but it was a difference. I think she was content, but I think she missed her farming." Her grandparents managed to maintain at least some of their former lifestyle.

Burnley Studevan remembers that "they used to make root beer soda in the basement. They used to make lye soap also. As a little girl, I used to love watching them make those things." Burnley Studevan's grandparents left behind a farm, but in Yeadon, they found a tightknit community. By 1940, 215 Black people resided in Yeadon. They lived in an area on Elder, Lincoln and Fairview Avenues and Providence Road, bordered to the west by Lansdowne Avenue and to the east by a wooded area. Yeadon's total population by this time numbered 8,524. The borough's White families largely resided outside of the Black enclave, abandoning the area as Black families moved in.

Home on Lincoln Avenue, one block away from Nile Swim Club of Yeadon. *Author's collection.*

Eloise Reed told the *Philadelphia Inquirer* in 1987 that her dad, Harvey M. Scott, a Pullman conductor and real estate speculator, purchased their house on Lincoln Avenue in 1933 and that a member of the White family that he bought the house from told her that they had to move because "they just never have lived next to colored people before." This was after another Black family had moved in next door.

Increasingly, Yeadon's West End promised Black families a chance to realize a suburban ideal denied elsewhere in the Philadelphia region and throughout much of the United States. For example, Audrey Brodie and her husband, a dentist in Chester, Pennsylvania, searched throughout Delaware County for a home to purchase prior to moving to Yeadon. She told the *Inquirer*, "They'd find out we were black and that would be that." When the Brodies found a house in Yeadon, then situated on an entirely White block, the real estate agent assured them that there would be no problems.

Soon after, their newly acquired space attracted vandals who tore out electrical fixtures, covered the place in dirt and wrote a racial slur on the wall. They moved in anyway and found themselves ignored by their White neighbors. Then one day, "a man knocked at her door to tell her the neighbors had a meeting and decided to sell their houses." He wanted to know if "she knew any professional 'Negroes'" who might be interested. Brodie "was so angry that I could hardly speak." The block became Black within a year.

The ones moving in persisted, determined to claim a space as their own, a suburb equal to any other. Though a struggle, they succeeded in historical fashion. According to the *Inquirer*, they "formed a black bedroom community that was such a rarity in the nation that magazines such as *Time* and *Ebony* published articles about it." Unaware of this as a child, Burnley Studevan did understand that "I was growing up with children whose parents all wanted the same thing for us. When I was home practicing violin, others were practicing piano. We were all doing about the same things."

Philadelphia's Black Main Line

In an article for the *New York Times*, "Black and Well-to-Do," Andrea Lee noted, "Our parents had a vision of pastoral normalcy for their children that was little different from the white ideal laid out in the Dick and Jane readers." Yeadon, she added, "was a great town to grow up in." Richard Guy told the *Inquirer*, "It was the black Main Line: living there meant you had made it." Denise Stewart Swann says, "We definitely had a lot of professional Blacks, but we also had people like my dad, who was a blue-collar worker. My father was a welder, but some of my best friends' fathers were doctors and lawyers. And the dads were all friends. They would get together at the pool to swim and play pinochle together."

At least initially, for some Whites who wandered into this emerging Black Main Line, it proved confusing. Eloise Reed told the *Philadelphia Inquirer* that White salesmen came to her family's house and routinely mistook her and her brother for house servants. When they learned that the "madam of the house" was a Black woman, it proved too much. They simply walked away. In East Yeadon, according to Jim Murphy, who grew up there, White children remained largely unaware that Black families lived on the other side of town. Murphy remembers that "our identity was closely bound to our school St. Louis, and the high school most attended, Monsignor Bonner," located in nearby Drexel Hill. As in West Yeadon, Murphy recalls that in East Yeadon, "our sense of community was ironclad." He observes, "The lives of Black and White people in Yeadon mirrored in virtually all respects, but they did not intersect."

According to the *Inquirer*, the ones who created Yeadon's Black enclave "might have stepped out of the pages of E. Franklin Frazier's 1957 book, *Black Bourgeoisie*," a chronicle of an emergent Black middle class. Ones who moved to Yeadon's West End in the 1940s, 1950s and 1960s include Robert "Bob" Bogle, then vice-president and treasurer of the *Philadelphia Tribune*; Tony Taylor and Richie "Dick" Allen, members of Major League Baseball's Philadelphia Phillies; and Leslie Pinkney Hill, president of Cheyney State University. On January 14, 1950, the *Philadelphia Tribune* ran the story "The Hasties at Home in Yeadon." It identified the Hasties as the family of U.S. Circuit Court judge William H. Hastie and featured a photo of them on the stairway of their new home at 83 Lincoln Avenue.

Hastie, a native of Knoxville, Tennessee, received his Doctor of Juridical Science degree from Harvard Law School in 1933. After working for the Department of the Interior, where he advised on racial issues, Hastie received appointment from President Franklin Delano Roosevelt to the District Court of the Virgin Islands. This made Hastie the first African American federal judge in United States history. After two years, he left the court to become the dean of the Howard University School of Law.

While there, Hastie taught Thurgood Marshall, the first Black justice appointed to the U.S. Supreme Court in 1967. With the outbreak of World War II, Hastie went back to work with the federal government, advocating from a post in the War Department for equal treatment of Black soldiers in America's military. He resigned his position in 1943 to protest the segregated training facilities maintained by the U.S. Army Air Forces.

Yeadon community leaders. *Nile Swim Club of Yeadon historical documents.*

That same year, in recognition of his dissent and to honor his lifetime achievements, the National Association for the Advancement of Colored People (NAACP) awarded Hastie its prestigious Spingarn Medal. Another presidential appointment brought Hastie to Yeadon. In 1949, President Harry S Truman named him to the U.S. Court of Appeals for the Third Circuit, located in Philadelphia. This made Hastie the first Black federal appellate judge in United States history and led President John F. Kennedy to consider nominating him to the Supreme Court.

After Hastie's passing in 1976, officials named the Third Circuit Court Library in his honor. Hastie's daughter Karen, five years old in the *Philadelphia Tribune*'s 1950 photo, became a prominent attorney and the first Black woman appointed clerk to a U.S. Supreme Court justice. The Hasties shared many characteristics with their neighbors on Yeadon's historic Black Main Line, a group that tripled in number since 1940, reaching 647 by 1950.

In 1987, the *Philadelphia Inquirer* observed about Yeadon that "most of the black residents were products of hard-working parents" who "instilled in them an overwhelming drive to succeed." Alice Roberson, whose family moved to Lincoln Avenue in 1959 from the Germantown neighborhood in Philadelphia, said, "My father wanted us to learn" and "he made sure that we did." Roberson's dad, Charles Fred White, an author and publisher, compiled a listing in 1912 of the one hundred most prominent Philadelphia Black people. Residents of Yeadon's West End, says the *Inquirer*, "took opera subscriptions, hired maids…and took extended leaves to study in Europe." They filled their homes with "antiques and objects of art collected on their travels."

Joseph William Harris, who frequented the Nile Swim Club as a kid, says, "I met so many people in this four-block area of my home, where the pool was only two blocks away. There were professionals, doctors and lawyers." Several of these constituted high-ranking Masons. Prohibited from joining the Freemasons, a fraternal organization dating back to the European Middle Ages, African Americans founded Prince Hall Freemasonry in 1784. Named after its founder, an eighteenth-century Black abolitionist and civil rights leader from Boston, Massachusetts, the Prince Hall Freemasons constitute the oldest and largest predominantly African American fraternity in the United States.

Growing up in Yeadon, Harris regularly interacted with thirty-three-degree Masons, Master Masons, designated by their fraternity for exhibiting "knowledge, passion and sacrifice" to one's craft and "selfless work" performed in public. Harris recalls knowing "at least six of them. There wasn't anywhere else in the country where there were that many Master Masons located in such a small proximity." That is, Harris says, "completely unusual." This constituted a group whose members possessed great confidence in their ability to reach any goal they set. "Movers and shakers," Harris suggests. "I guess that is what you'd call them."

Cold War Context

In post–World War II America, a bipartisan Cold War consensus emerged that exerted political pressure on both Whites and Blacks to embrace a conservative, anticommunist Americanism. Black people pressing for radical change proved especially vulnerable to being identified by authorities as Communists. Both *Jet* magazine and *Ebony* magazine, founded after World War II ended, glamorized a White consumerist ideal, newly attainable, they posited, to their readers. This carrot, combined with the stick wielded by Senator Joseph R. McCarthy to generate a Red Scare, pressured a centering of Black political culture, away from earlier New Deal ideas.

Much of the promise for entering the "power elite," as sociologist C. Wright Mills dubbed it in his 1956 bestseller by the same name, proved hollow. Following America's victory over fascism during the Second World War, America's "Negro Problem" increasingly garnered the attention of United States allies and emerged immediately as a chief theme of Soviet propaganda. This presented United States officials with a tremendous obstacle in competing with Communists in the resource-rich Black, Brown and Asian postcolonial world.

Historian Mary Dudziak demonstrated in *Cold War Civil Rights: Race and the Image of American Democracy* that the Cold War helped facilitate social reforms, but "improving the nation's international reputation did not always require real change." She argued that the "focus on image rather than substance—combined with constraints on McCarthy-era political activism and the triumph of law-and-order rhetoric—limited the nature and extent of progress." Yeadon reflected this, an extension of "separate but equal," once the school day ended at integrated Yeadon High.

The situation at Yeadon High suggested a sort of détente, a term describing an accepted, if superficial, "peaceful coexistence" internationally between the Communist and noncommunist blocs. In Yeadon, détente applied to race rather than ideology—if everybody stayed on their side of Church Lane, in their own local blocs. Father Logan, the neighbor of Joseph William Harris, emerged as one of Yeadon's "movers and shakers" who navigated the contours of America's Cold War consensus effectively. He did so on a national stage.

He became a force for equality, regionally, nationally and globally. Born in 1912, Reverend Canon Thomas Wilson Stearly Logan Sr. died in 2012 at the age of one hundred. He attained the distinction of being the oldest serving African American priest in the Episcopal Church. It proved a distinguished tenure. As the *Philadelphia Tribune* identified in his obituary, Logan received five honorary doctorates through the course of his life.

During the civil rights movement, Logan collaborated with Dr. Martin Luther King Jr. in organizational fundraising and strategic efforts. His leadership resonated widely, including in his capacity as one of the founders of the African American Museum in Philadelphia. The city's mayor, Michael Nutter, said that Logan's "service to the community, to the nation, and I would suggest to the world, has really been something to admire." He continued to suggest that "any one of us should hope to do so much, and to live so long."

Jason N. Calhoun, another resident of West Yeadon, additionally made his mark on the world. A resident of 28 East Providence Road, Calhoun served as the director of planning for the Health and Welfare Council of Philadelphia. He came to that position as a graduate of Samuel Huston College in Austin, Texas, and the University of Michigan School of Public Health. He worked in hospital administration in the South Pacific during World War II and then became a faculty member of the Texas State School for the Deaf and Blind. On December 22, 1953, the *Philadelphia Tribune* reported that Calhoun became one of twenty-three technicians selected by the United States government for overseas assignment with the Foreign Operations Administration. He received a posting to Baghdad, Iraq, with the United States Operations Mission as a public health educator.

Another resident of West Yeadon, Myers L. Thomas, became president of H.R.I. Management Inc. In 1991, President George H.W. Bush nominated his brother Clarence to fill Thurgood Marshall's seat on the U.S. Supreme Court. Clarence Thomas received confirmation to become the second Black Supreme Court justice. That transpired, however, only after Senate confirmation hearings took place that centered on the accusation that he sexually harassed attorney Anita Hill, a subordinate of his while he earlier chaired the Equal Employment Opportunity Commission under President Ronald W. Reagan. A neighbor of Myers Thomas, Lamont Ferrell remembers, "during that whole Anita Hill thing, the news media came and interviewed us because he didn't want to talk to them!"

Neighborhood Politics

While some Whites resisted the construction of Yeadon's Black enclave, the ones who resided there endeavored to succeed in their professions and in building their community. The West Yeadon Civic Association, "which started as a garden club," according to the *Philadelphia Inquirer*, became "so strong that developers often would throw in the towel after learning that the association was opposed to a particular project." The association worked assiduously to maintain the integrity of West Yeadon's neighborly environment.

On November 5, 1955, the *Philadelphia Tribune* reported that West Yeadon Civic Association president Kermit J. Hall presented Yeadon's Borough Council with a petition signed by nearly three hundred residents that protested a proposed zoning change in West Yeadon's rating from B-residential to light industry. Era J. Rodgers, the civic association's secretary, told the *Tribune* that "this proposed change would decrease the values and the sales of new houses which are in great demand by Negroes in the area." She said, "Yeadon is a residential borough, and the people want to keep it that way." The association, over the years, kept vigilant to ensure that this stayed the case.

More than twenty years later, in 1978, the association again opposed the zoning board to "retain the existing character of the neighborhood." In this case, on June 6, the *Philadelphia Tribune* cited the proposal of Bodek Enterprises as the instigating factor. Bodek wished to build at least six new houses along Wycomb Avenue between Providence Road and Lincoln Avenue. These lacked the required footage, a fifty-foot front and a one-hundred-foot depth, for the number of dwellings. The West Yeadon Civic Association made its case successfully to the zoning board, limiting construction to no more than four or five properties that "would not impose congestion on the residential area." Despite Joseph Bodek's protest, the board found that his initial proposal "failed to demonstrate that six homes would not alter the character of the neighborhood."

The association further worked routinely to support the educational experience of West Yeadon's students. On May 12, 1959, for example, the West Yeadon Civic Association announced the upcoming of its annual spring dance, "A May Fiesta." Under the direction of Mrs. Byron Reed Sr., the association planned to turn the main ballroom of the Yeadon Borough Hall into "a scene of enchantment and color." The event aimed to benefit the association's annual awards for the Yeadon High School graduating class.

A sense of community permeated West Yeadon. On January 15, 1952, the *Philadelphia Tribune* reported that the residents of Providence Road and Elder Avenue recently "enjoyed the hospitality of Mr. and Mrs. Arthur Green when the Greens staged a 'get together' party." According to the *Tribune*, the Greens "broke the ice" and invited some of their new neighbors in for an evening of "relaxation and buffet supper." This marked the couple's second year living in their Yeadon home. They said, "We found a home just made for us, and we could not have any better neighbors."

All the Greens desired, they explained, "is more opportunities to be neighborly and more cooperation in making our community the kind that we would like to live in." The Greens and their neighbors succeeded, according to Denise Stewart Swann. She says, "I feel so blessed to have grown up in Yeadon. We could keep our door open at night and have no fear. I walk to my friends' houses, or my church near Lansdowne, and have no fear. And I had a lot of good friends who are White; we're still in touch today." In "Black and Well-to-Do," Andrea Lee called Yeadon "the kind of town few people believe exists: a black upper middle class suburb." She said, "Childhood in Yeadon was a suburban idyll of shady streets and bicycles and ice cream from a drugstore called Doc's."

Suburban Living

On April 26, 1955, the *Philadelphia Tribune* reported that "Yeadon's Negro home ownership percentage is one of the highest in the United States." It noted, "More than 90 percent of the Negroes living in this sleepy nearby Delaware County village own their own homes." To put that into perspective, in 2020 the homeownership rate for Black Americans stood at 43.4 percent, according to a study by the National Association of Realtors (NAR). That is nearly thirty percentage points lower than White homeownership, around 72.1 percent.

Black homeownership additionally ranked lower than that of both Asian Americans (61.7 percent) and Hispanic Americans (51.1 percent). Mortgage lenders rejected 7 percent of Black loan applications, a rate nearly double that of Whites (4 percent). The NAR study reports that nearly one-third of Black respondents faced stricter requirements because of their race. The same number, 32 percent, said that they witnessed or experienced racial discrimination with the type of loan offer they received.

The historically high proportion of Black homeownership in Yeadon resulted from a "financing arrangement," cited by the *Philadelphia Tribune* on November 22, 1941, as one "that seems almost miraculous." The newspaper credited it with placing a "large number of semi-detached homes" in Yeadon "within the reach of any family with a modest income." Located at Union and Fairview Avenues, the houses sold for $2,990. This required a $290 cash down payment and a loan that cost $27 per month for eleven years and seven months.

Each home possessed three bedrooms, a tile bath, living room, dining room and kitchen, garage in the basement, hot water heat and hardwood floors. The homes enjoyed privacy provided by "large English hedges," while "many of the yards," the *Tribune* described, "are bordered with tall poplars and weeping willow trees." The *Tribune* touted Yeadon as offering easy access to Philadelphia and "other ideal conditions such as conservative families for neighbors, fine schools, and beautiful landscaping." The paper urged prospective buyers to contact S.J. McCracken, located on Lancaster Avenue, "the exclusive agent."

In the weeks that followed, the *Tribune* inspected the homes and reported its findings to its readers. On December 6, 1941, the newspaper announced, "Seeing is believing, after all—so when the ultra-modern and beautiful homes in Yeadon, Pennsylvania, were recently placed on sale to Negroes by S.J. McCracken, Inc., a reporter was assigned to travel out there to make an informal inspection." They liked what they saw. The article described "arriving at the sample house at 154 Fairview avenue it was obvious…that the developers of this newest community had shown a close regard for the latest and most convenient trend in present day interior planning." It called the living room the "piece de resistance," representing the "embodiment of the dream of every prospective homeowner." It featured a red brick open fireplace accented by a very wide painted panel.

The home tour continued up a "wide and graceful staircase" to explore the second-floor bedrooms. The master bedroom "boasted a well arranged deep closet, polished hardwood floors and gleaming white woodwork, not to mention two extremely large windows." The other two bedrooms proved "equally attractive." The second-floor hallway then ended "in a large sunny bathroom with tiled walls and a floor of white marble, and the very latest in plumbing fixtures." Returning then to the first floor, "the reporter passed through a large dining room" and into a "very adequate kitchen…perfectly contrasted by its maroon colored inlaid linoleum floor." The kitchen featured "modern fixtures" while offering access down a set of stairs into the garage.

Besides the reporter's description of the sample house, the *Tribune* offered accounts from homeowners in the neighborhood. It reported that "Mrs. Anton Harris who lives at 172 Fairview avenue could hardly find words with which to express her joy at being able to live in such a perfect home." She praised the "reasonable arrangements" for payment that "are so easy for a family with a moderate income to comply with." She said that her family looked forward to "many long, happy and cozy winter days and evenings," rendered possible by the hot water heating system that promises "great comfort." Another neighbor raved about "the fact that her home, although placed in a section where one is assured peace and quiet is still easily accessible to the city."

Yeadon's Black Main Line contained great promise, one that it realized for its residents. As Andrea Lee observed in 1982 for the *New York Times*, "Yes Virginia, there is a black bourgeoisie." These "black professionals were as eager as anyone else at that time to pursue the romantic suburban dream of field stone patios and eye level ovens. By the 1950s, half the black doctors and lawyers in Philadelphia crowded into this rather small town." More precisely, they moved into the West End of that town. The rest of the borough, despite the stature of West Yeadon's occupants, remained off limits. The Black Main Line's realization arrived with a sharply drawn racial perimeter.

MASON-DIXON LINES

That Was Their Side

Black residents participated in public groups, working with Whites on Yeadon's school board, the Parent Teacher Association (PTA) and the library board. Otherwise, however, Church Lane, Yeadon's main thoroughfare, became the unofficial border between the town's Black and White communities. Some Black residents referred to it as Yeadon's "Mason-Dixon line," referencing the dividing line between America's slave owning South and the free North prior to the Civil War. Alice Roberson told the *Philadelphia Inquirer*, "We didn't even think about living over there. That was their side." Norman Miller recalls, "Once you crossed over Church Lane, it was all White. West Yeadon was our little island. Back then, it was a weird place."

Activities other than home buying also proved restricted. The restaurant on Church Lane that proved popular with White students did not welcome their Black peers. Yvonne Burnley Studevan remembers, "It was difficult because the White kids would go to Don's after school, but the Black kids had no place to go." She laughs, "Some kids would then just go out and meet on the street corner, but I could not do that; my parents were the kind to say, 'You come home from school, you come into the house.'" Some, however, managed to congregate at Matt-Matt's, a steak shop located at Wycombe and Providence. Bill Mellix Jr. recalls that is where he went to "hang out with the boys."

Protest against the family of Horace Baker moving into previously all-White neighborhood in Folcroft, Pennsylvania, near Yeadon in Delaware County, August 1963. *Library of Congress.*

Burnley Studevan had White friends at school, but that is where the relationships remained. "They stayed in their community," she says, "and I stayed in mine. It was very segregated, out of school." Burnley Studevan does remember at least one exception, "a little girl by the name of Mary Jane Hood, and she invited me to her home." Burnley Studevan accepted the invitation and then extended one of her own. She remembers, "When it came time to take Mary Jane back to her house, my mother said to my aunt, 'Do you think Mary Jane's parents know that Yvonne is Black?'" Her aunt replied, "Well they'll know when I take her home." The two childhood friends remained close until Hood passed away in 2018.

Lauretta Miller observes, "We had to be very careful; the neighboring communities were lily white." According to Joseph William Harris, "There were places you couldn't go at a certain time." He adds, though, "Yeadon wasn't as bad as the rest of Delaware County." Denise Stewart Swann says, "We would go to [neighboring] Upper Darby during the day to go shopping on 69th Street, but after that, we didn't go anywhere else in Upper Darby." Stewart Swann adds, "We definitely did not go to Clifton Heights. We knew we were not wanted there."

Stewart Swann recalls her few times in Clifton Heights as a cheerleader for Yeadon's high school football team. "When we would cheer at games at

Clifton Heights, they would throw things at us. It was bad. A bad situation that got to the point where the administration wouldn't even let us go anymore. They feared for our safety, the Black students." Such experiences outside Yeadon fostered the perception of West Yeadon as a safe place, one that offered whatever one might need.

About Yeadon's divide, Karen Hall Eskridge says, "I didn't equate it to segregation or separation. It's just that our folks didn't feel like they needed to fight to fit in to the White end. When I was coming up, in the '60s, I never ventured to Church Lane. I didn't need to. It was like, 'Hey, we're all educated, we've got good jobs, our kids go to the same school; if we can have our own, we have our own." And their own West Yeadon constituted a special space. But the children of its residents, able to attend Yeadon High School, received clear notice that the Yeadon Swim Club remained off limits. It remained exclusively White, hosting splash parties for children and featuring local entertainers such as Bobby Darin and Jerry Blavat. Of course, the Yeadon Swim Club also offered swimming lessons. Jim Murphy frequented the club as a kid and remembers that "none of our parents could swim." He says that they all came from neighborhoods in West Philadelphia, where "the only water available in the summer came from opened fire hydrants." As a resulted, they insisted that their kids learn to swim.

Segregated Swim Clubs

Other private swim clubs nearby were similar, constructed by Whites after the Supreme Court's decision in 1954 that mandated the desegregation of public schools. Organizers sought to take advantage of federal law that permitted private clubs to establish their own membership criteria. On these grounds, the Yeadon Swim Club remained segregated until it closed in 2000 for failure to pay taxes. At that time, Jacquelynn Puriefoy-Brinkley, daughter of one of the Nile Swim Club's founders, Carson Puriefoy, presided over Yeadon's Borough Council. Shuttering the Yeadon Swim Club marked the first time she or any other Black individual went inside. In 2009, she told the *Philadelphia Inquirer* that she felt no sense of triumph, only "a sweep of emotion so overpowering that she had to escape." She hurried out the door.

More recently, in an interview, Puriefoy-Brinkley explained that the Yeadon Swim Club could not pay its taxes because "they refused to expand their membership by allowing Blacks in." So, she said, "I was president of Borough Council and I made sure we bought that Swim Club. I didn't want anybody else to build another swim club that would be competition to the Nile. So, we bought it." Then, following a pause, she laughs, "And we killed it." Before they did, though, Puriefoy-Brinkley adds, "We got everything we could from that Swim Club. The director of Public Works lined up the borough trucks. He was a White guy, but he knew what had happened. He also knew that Public Works did the landscaping for that club…while we were paying taxes and they didn't do anything for the Nile Swim Club."

Justice of sorts finally came to Yeadon, as it did in neighboring Lansdowne. On July 2, 1989, the *Philadelphia Inquirer* reported that federal justice Thomas N. O'Neil Jr. ruled that the Lansdowne Swim Club "engaged in a pattern or practice of discrimination against blacks." According to the *Inquirer*, since it opened, the Lansdowne Club approved the applications of more than one thousand White families, while rejecting only two. It received applications from six Black families during that time and rejected them all. The ruling came thirty-two years after the Swim Club opened its doors in 1957 and resulted from suit filed in the U.S. District Court in Philadelphia by three Lansdowne families, the Ryans, the Allisons and the Iverys. Lisa Ivery, daughter of one Ellen Ivery who joined the suit, remembers how it all happened.

The Iverys lived in the Black section of predominantly White Lansdowne, immediately adjacent to West Yeadon. As a child, Lisa played many sports, often with mostly White teammates. She remembers that after practices in the summer, many of her White friends would talk about "going swimming at the Club." She thought at the time, "Why don't I ever get invited?" The family of Lisa's friends, Anita and Vivian Allison, attempted to join the Lansdowne Swim Club. Lisa says, "Their mom, Dale, was White. Their dad, Dr. Allison, was Black." She continues, "From my memory, they were the first to try and join the Swim Club; it was near their house." The Lansdowne Swim Club responded by waitlisting the Allisons, even as it admitted families who applied after they did. Lisa explains, "Other people were joining no problem. But every time the Allisons checked on their application, the club responded by saying, 'Oh we are so sorry, so sorry, but we don't have any open memberships.'"

Lisa says that her mom, Ellen, and Dale Allison "were very close." She continues, "The story that I remember is that the group of people ready to tackle the Lansdowne Swim Club said my mom was the perfect one to try and join.

The reasons for that assessment included Ellen Ivery's activist spirit, one she channeled for her children. Lisa remembers that when she attended elementary school, they closed the nearby school she attended on Green Avenue. Officials informed parents that students now would attend school on Ardmore Avenue, "which is way on the other side of Lansdowne." Lisa notes, "That was probably the first time that my mom, and other moms, became really active."

This occurred as a result of a decree by school officials, one that called for elementary-aged children from south Lansdowne to walk, about a mile, to their new school on Ardmore Avenue. Lisa says, "They thought it was okay for us, little kids, to walk all that way back and forth to school every day." That prompted Lisa's mom to work with other parents to orchestrate a bus boycott. Lisa remembers, "They barricaded the bus depot. They said if our kids aren't getting a bus, then nobody is getting a bus. A lot of the Black mothers from south Lansdowne did this because that is who it was impacting." Ivery laughs, "My brother was still in a stroller, but my mother said, 'We're going up there!'" Ivery notes, "That's the first memory I have of my mom bucking up, saying we aren't going to put up with any nonsense from anybody. And we ended up getting buses."

Besides Ellen Ivery's activist spirit, the group standing with the Allisons understood that people at the Lansdowne Club all knew her. Lisa explains, "My mom was active in the community helping other parents out. She often drove my friends whose families belonged to the club back and forth from games, practices and Girl Scout events." The group thought, "It's not like she [Ellen Ivery] is an outsider. They can't say they don't know what she is about. Let's send her there and see if she can get in. She should be able to get in." This resulted, according to Lisa, "in the same thing. The club said it had no open memberships." She notes, "That's how the whole thing got started. That's when the lawsuit was filed, because at this point, the club is telling my mom no and the Allisons no, and for what reason? We all only had one thing in common, that is we were Black." She adds, "It was really kind of obvious."

At the Lansdowne Swim Club, that option did not exist, intentionally and from the beginning, according to one of the club's founders Matthew Richards. In reporting on the suit, the *Inquirer* noted that in court Matthew Richards testified that when the founders raised money for the pool's construction, they did so by going door to door avoiding the "black parts of town." If Black families expressed interest, they told them to apply to the Nile. U.S. Department of Justice attorney Harvey I. Handley III observed in court testimony, according to the *Inquirer*, that members of the Lansdowne Swim Club "do not object to blacks per se. It is only blacks that apply to the club that they find unacceptable." That validated the perception of the club long held by Anita Allison, daughter of one who filed suit, Dale Allison. She informed the *Inquirer* that she lost interest in the Swim Club in the third grade. That is when her friends remarked, "I could probably get you in, pass you off as Italian."

Despite the ruling in favor of the group that filed suit, Lisa Ivery says, "I've never even been in that club." She explains, "There's just something still in me at fifty-four years old that when I drive by that place I just cringe." Ivery adds, "I've never even driven into the driveway. I see their sign, and there is a part of me that is still irritated. You know what I mean?" She offers, "Now, of course, they have to let African Americans in there, but I'm sure they don't know what happened. And I'm sure it is a limited quantity. They still are not going to let Black folks come in there and take over the club." All of it, Ivery says, "still irks me."

The decision against the Lansdowne Swim Club required it to place an advertisement in a Delaware County newspaper proclaiming, "All persons may become a member of the Lansdowne Swim Club without regard to race or color." That never transpired in Yeadon, as nobody sued. They simply went to the Nile—the place that welcomed them, the space that felt comfortable. That included Lisa Ivery. She found the Nile to be a haven. She says, "I was there every day, from the time it opened until it closed." Even rain made no difference. Ivery said simply, "Oh, it's raining, I'm still in the water! Oh, it's thundering, okay, I'll get out, but I'm getting back in after forty-five minutes." She adds, "I was an all-day kid. In the summer, I wanted to be there all the time." She remembers telling her mother on morning

Ellen F. Ivery (*left*) and daughter Lisa M. Ivery. *Lisa Ivery.*

shopping trips, "Fine, I'll go, but I've got my bathing suit on and you need to drop me at the pool by noon."

In Lansdowne, the court ruled that the Swim Club did not constitute a "selective private club," but instead existed as a public accommodation, much like a restaurant. The Yeadon Swim Club's status remained unchallenged, however, and it continued to discriminate by race. Nile Swim Club president Anthony Patterson Sr. remembers that Cal Puriefoy played basketball on a Yeadon High team and so earned an invitation to the Yeadon Swim Club. This constitutes the first and only time a Black person received an invitation to the Swim Club on the other side of town. When he arrived at the club with his teammates, however, his coach greeted him at the gate and said, "'I'm sorry Cal, but you can't come in.' The coach actually told him that. They sent Cal home, and all the White players went in. And that was in the late '70s, early '80s."

Wanda Reese, who grew up across the street from the Nile, recalls, "I didn't even realize I wasn't welcome at another pool. I didn't realize there was somewhere else to swim in Yeadon." She says, "Either my classmates did not talk about it or I was just oblivious, I don't know." But what Reese does know is "that was the whole reason that this pool was built, so I wouldn't have to feel that way, unwelcome because of my race." Kathleen Wainwright adds, "Well, I know in the '80s I had Black friends that lived on the other side of Yeadon that got turned away." She continues, "I didn't even know there was a pool over there, that it was still open. It didn't matter." Karen Hall Eskridge says, "Y'know the funny thing was, when I was in junior high and high school, in the 1960s, some of the folks I hung out with, they weren't allowed at the Yeadon pool either because they were Jewish. So, most of them had their own pools."

According to Lamont Ferrell, a teenager in the early 1980s, "We were very aware of the Yeadon Swim Club. Nobody ever said that you couldn't go there. You just knew you couldn't. It was forbidden." Ferrell remembers coming and going from basketball practice, passing by the Yeadon Swim Club. "You would see all your friends headed in there," he says, "in all their summer gear, with their floats and stuff for the pool. Then when you saw your White classmates at lunch in school, you would hear all about the swim parties and stuff." Ferrell adds, "But you knew you were you. You were going to the Nile on the other side of town. So, y'know, it was definitely segregated. Like two separate worlds almost." Looking back, he says, "It was just ignorance."

Of course, not everybody remembers it that way. When the Nile Swim Club celebrated its thirtieth anniversary in 1989, former Yeadon mayor Nick D'Alessandro, an original member of the Yeadon Swim Club, told the *Philadelphia Inquirer* that the Black residents of West Yeadon "were not denied." Instead, they "just wanted to have their own swim club." D'Alessandro remained "under the impression that they wanted their own pool" because "they were lawyers, doctors and so on." That impression proved mistaken. As the *Philadelphia Daily News* reported in 2008, "No one said they [African Americans] couldn't join the Yeadon Swim Club. Racism didn't work that way in 1950s Yeadon, Delaware County. Rather than saying no, town officials said nothing."

Racist Walls

But the silence spoke loudly. Founder Carlson Puriefoy's daughter Jacquelynn remembers her father filling out a Yeadon Swim Club application at borough hall. After stepping away, Puriefoy returned to complete the form. "When he went back to amend it," she recalls, "they fetched his application out of the trash can for him." It is hard to imagine a more demeaning reception, particularly for one so devoted to humanitarian reform. Clearly, Yeadon Swim Club officials knew little about Carson Puriefoy. His children recall his mantra for the family: "When you come to the brick wall, you go through it."

Born in 1915, Carson Puriefoy came to the Elmwood neighborhood of Philadelphia from Griffin, Georgia, just before turning six years old. This derived from a dispute with a White neighbor in Georgia over a cow. While what exactly happened remains unclear, it caused Carson's older brother, a World War I veteran, to pull out an old gun. Afraid that he might use this, the family prevailed on Carson's brother for them all to pack up in the middle of the night. They left behind whatever they could not carry, including their land. In Elmwood, they initially settled into a hotel. Soon after, they found jobs, went to work and set about constructing homes.

The Puriefoy family experience is not unique. Goin' North: Stories from the First Great Migration to Philadelphia, a collection of oral histories and digital storytelling compiled by Charles Hardy and Janneken Smucker with their students at West Chester University, renders this evident. The project explains, "Between 1910 and 1930, the African-American population of Philadelphia skyrocketed, from around 85,000 to nearly 220,000 in the early years of the Great Depression." This resulted from those "who left lives behind in the South and ventured north in search of opportunity and equality, pushed out by the increasingly hostile environment of Jim Crow racism." The name "Jim Crow" derived from a Black minstrel show character and referred to the strict racial segregation laws enacted throughout the American South following the end of post–Civil War Reconstruction.

Jim Crow constituted a systemic tool of oppression, one indiscriminately wielded in the White South. Arkansas native Crosby Brittenum, born in 1899, came to Philadelphia in 1920. He told oral historian Charles Hardy during a 1984 interview posted on Goin' North, "They used to treat colored people terribly bad in Mississippi and Alabama. Them two states. And Georgia. They were pretty hard. You know, they used to practically lynch—lynch colored people for—you might well say for looking at a White woman." The threat of mob justice, ultra-violent and arbitrary, loomed continuously over southern Black people. It often materialized suddenly and became cause for immediate flight.

This served as the impetus for Kathryn F. ("Kitty") Woodward and her family's journey to Philadelphia in 1921. She explained to Hardy in a 1984, "I guess, when I was five years old, my father came home one night and told my mother he was in a hurry....And she said, 'What's wrong?' And he told her that he had to get Uncle Leon out quickly, because it was a mob gonna try to lynch him. He said, 'Because the only thing is this White woman's word that he was bothering her.'"

Philadelphia, the "City of Brotherly Love," appeared a place that promised southern Black families racial equality. Like other northern cities, it often failed to deliver. Historian Jeffrey Wiltse, a contributor to *Pool: A Social History of Segregation*, observed that "the first wave of the Great Black Migration intensified other racist prejudices." Jim Crow's shadow extended easily beyond the Mason-Dixon line.

In Philadelphia, as a result of the Great Migration, racial and ethnically homogenous neighborhoods emerged to coexist uneasily, governed by unwritten rules. Brittenum explained to Hardy that "certain parts we couldn't go. And, uh, certain parts they couldn't go, you know, because that's the way the colored would get back at them, if one of them come back in the colored neighborhood, they'd—they'd do things to him. We got in the White neighborhood; they'd do things to us. So they avoid that, you know. It...was like that."

But it became unavoidable as overcrowding resulted in Black families increasingly moving into neighborhoods formerly White. In July 1918, for example, White neighbors in the 2500 block of Philadelphia's Pine Street attacked the homes of two Black families. Riots ensued that left four persons dead and several hundred injured. While Whites initiated the incident, the police predominantly arrested Blacks. The *Philadelphia Tribune* blamed this on law enforcement, accusing Philadelphia's police department of refusing to protect the property of Black residents. The *Tribune*'s G. Grant Williams asked why "police arrest a colored man or woman for protecting their home?…The colored people of Philadelphia are law abiding citizens…if you don't protect them, they shall and will defend themselves."

The tensions, as historians Raymond B. Hyser and Dennis B. Downey suggested in "A Crooked Death: Coatesville Pennsylvania and the Death of Zachariah Walker," resulted in the receiving "brunt of the New Immigration [southern and eastern Europeans] and the Great Migration of southern Blacks simultaneously." White nativist backlash proved severe. On August 12, 1911, African American steelworker Zachariah Walker, after a day spent drinking, fired his handgun twice into the air while stumbling home along a darkened road. Edgar Rice, a Worth Brothers Steel police officer, heard the shots and accosted Walker.

The incident escalated, both drew guns and Rice ended up dead. Walker evaded authorities until the next day. A group of firefighters tried to apprehend him, but Walker shot himself in the jaw in an unsuccessful suicide attempt. He was taken into custody, where he confessed to the shooting but insisted that it was an act of self-defense. When the town's population learned that authorities admitted Walker into the Coatesville hospital to recover, a mob of about two thousand took Walker from his room and burned him to death on a makeshift funeral pyre. State and national authorities, including President Theodore Roosevelt, condemned the lynching, and the State of Pennsylvania conducted a probe of the incident that resulted in six indictments; all eventually received acquittals.

Walker's lynching counted as the eighth, and the last known, in Pennsylvania. It also resulted in legislation that made lynching a state crime. This hardly resulted in racial equality. In fact, Pennsylvania's state legislature rejected an equal rights bill introduced in 1921 by John C. Asbury, a Black Republican representative from Philadelphia. There remained many barriers, placed systemically and strategically, aimed to thwart Black progress. They failed to disappear over time, including those brick walls that Carson Puriefoy urged his children, decades later, to continue pushing against. His experience provided them a model.

You Had to Be the Best

Once he arrived in Philadelphia, Puriefoy attended public school, graduating from Bartram High School. He then earned a degree from the University of Pennsylvania's Wharton School of Business. In 1935, at the age of twenty, Puriefoy became the first African American manager for American Stores Inc., now Acme Supermarkets. Puriefoy's daughter Jacquelynn reflects, "I think it was true for him, other Blacks who came from the South, this mentality that you had to succeed. You had to be the best. That's how it was."

It is no coincidence that Puriefoy's daughter Wendy took a degree in history. Her parents routinely made it Black history—American history. When Carson Puriefoy passed away in 1995 at the age of eighty years old, the *Philadelphia Tribune* praised him as a "trailblazer in several arenas of life." Puriefoy soon left his job to partner with his brother in opening businesses, including their own supermarket in Eastwick, Philadelphia's southwesternmost neighborhood, adjacent to the Philadelphia International Airport.

Puriefoy additionally worked for Wyeth Ayrst Pharmaceuticals as a regional manager. According to the *Tribune*, while working in that capacity, he became an "early advocate for low cost generic drugs." He additionally combined forces with his wife, Betty, a pioneering and dynamic Black woman. Of her parents, Jacquelynn Puriefoy-Brinkley recalls, "They were the most wonderful parents that kids could have. They wanted us to know that we could accomplish anything that we wanted."

Born in Wachaprague, Virginia, in 1915, the same year as her husband, Betty G. Puriefoy grew up in Georgia. No public high schools for Black children existed nearby, so her parents sent her to the Eastern Shore of Maryland, where she attended Princess Anne Academy, a teacher preparation school and forerunner of Maryland State College, now the University of Maryland Eastern Shore. She earned her teacher certificate there and became a passionate educator and civic leader. She served on several committees that awarded scholarships to Black youths and became a leader in the West Yeadon Civic Association, where she helped found Town Watch.

When Betty G. Puriefoy died in 1992, the *Philadelphia Tribune* commented, "Her determination to exercise her right to express her opinion to anyone in a position of influence led to ongoing correspondence with the late U.S. Senator and Vice President Hubert H. Humphrey and former President Jimmy Carter." It added, "She and Humphrey became close friends." For much of her life, Betty G. Puriefoy confronted a Mason-Dixon line that proved unsafe to cross in her own hometown.

The Puriefoys had four children: Jacquelynn, Carson, Dale and Wendy. The family first lived in Philadelphia before moving to Yeadon, where they became beloved members of the community—especially Dale, perhaps. Jacquelynn says, "My brother was handicapped; he had been damaged at birth. But my parents were determined that Dale would lead a normal life. They were told that Dale would never read. Well, Dale went to the library every Saturday and came home with at least four books. Dale was a real giver in this community, and people loved him." Joseph William Harris says of Dale, "He was the best friend you could ever have."

And once the Nile Swim Club opened, Harris remembers, "He managed to do the security of the pool better than anybody you could ever hire. Dale was the kind of person that whenever the pool doors opened, he was there doing whatever they needed him to do." He proved especially adept at managing the parking lot. According to Harris, "His speech was a little different…it was a little slower, so you had to really listen to what he was saying. And I think he knew that. He would speak intentionally in a rhythmic way that you couldn't get mad at him. You'd want to listen to him because you knew he was trying to say something. And he would never get excited, but he would not leave until you did what he asked you to do."

In fact, Harris adds, "The police even used him for Town Watch." Active in the community, Dale Puriefoy took a job at the U.S. Postal Service, where he worked until his retirement. Dale Puriefoy's job resulted from the conviction of his parents to help him along with others like him. Carson and Betty Puriefoy proved instrumental in establishing the first sheltered workshop for people with mental disabilities in Delaware County. They additionally acted as founding members of the Delaware County Association for Retarded and Handicapped Children.

Chicken Bone Beach

Other businesses established by Carson Puriefoy included a cafeteria in Yeadon's industrial park, one that ensured that "workers there could get a hot lunch," according to Harris. He also ventured into a business in Atlantic City, New Jersey. This rendered him familiar with "Chicken Bone Beach." It is a place many of the Nile Swim Club's members remember well, Bill Mellix Jr. included. He notes that although "it wasn't all of Atlantic City, it was Missouri Avenue, that was Chicken Bone Beach. And they called it Chicken Bone Beach because we took chicken down to the beach."

To escape their city's stifling heat and humidity during the summer, Philadelphians had long journeyed to New Jersey's shore. This remains a popular pastime with families, annually vacationing at their traditional spots along the coast like the Wildwoods, Margate and Ocean City. Black Philadelphians do the same, but for much of the twentieth century, Chicken Bone Beach represented the only possible destination. As Mellix Jr. recalls, "We didn't go to Wildwood. We didn't go to Cape May or Margate or any of those; Blacks went to Atlantic City." There existed a historical Black community there that enabled a unique African American presence on the Jersey shore. Of Chicken Bone Beach, Denise Stewart Swann recalls, "That was basically the only beach we could go to."

This remained limited, however, as Atlantic City enforced strict segregation. This gave the beach its name. The Black families who frequented it discovered that "chicken lasted longer in the heat than other foods," as historian Cheryl Woodruff-Brooks explained in *Chicken Bone Beach: A Pictorial History of Atlantic City's Missouri Avenue Beach*. Black beachgoers to Atlantic City discovered this out of necessity. As Woodruff-Brooks observed, "Since African Americans were not permitted to eat in the restaurants on the boardwalk, they packed their own food and brought it to the beach." When cleaning the beach's sand, Atlantic City employees regularly found chicken bones, discarded by beachgoers and pulled up by seagulls seeking a meal. Still, as Woodruff-Brooks wrote, "Not every resident is fond of the nickname…some perceived it to be an insult and as a means of stereotyping their race."

"What's interesting about Atlantic City," Woodruff Brooks observed, "is that in many ways, racial separation did not exist" in its early history. "Blacks and Whites owned homes wherever they wanted to." About 70 percent of Black people in Atlantic City lived next door to Whites in the 1880s. Within twenty years, as Atlantic City grew as a resort town and attracted Black migrants with jobs, the number dropped to 20 percent. If not already present, Jim Crow followed Black migrants wherever they went, even to places that already contained significant Black populations.

"A Beach Scene." *New York Public Library Digital Collections.*

This proved especially to be the case in Atlantic City, a tourist town marketed to Whites, including ones who arrived there to vacation from places less diverse. They enjoyed the service provided by Black staff and attended the performances of Black entertainers, but they expressed no interest in seeing Black people elsewhere. This included the beach as well as Atlantic City's only swimming pool. They tolerated Chicken Bone Beach only because the Million Dollar Pier, an entertainment strip, blocked its view from the boardwalk, which remained accessible only to Whites.

Even if they were pushed out of sight, Atlantic City emerged as a premier vacation spot for Black families, largely because it represented one of the few safe places in the country to relax. This is reflected in its favorable listing in *The Green Book*, a travel guide created by New York postal worker Victor Hugo Green in 1936. He published new editions throughout the 1960s to help African Americans, increasingly automobile owners, identify where they might travel comfortably and safely. Atlantic City's large Black population, concentrated in the Northside, developed a vibrant nightlife that regularly featured top-notch Black entertainers.

Club Harlem, for example, a one-thousand-seat venue located on Kentucky Avenue, welcomed performers such as Aretha Franklin, Sam Cooke and James Brown. While White Atlantic City remained off limits to Blacks, Whites regularly frequented Kentucky Avenue without incident. Bill Mellix Jr. recalls, "Before the casinos opened, there were a lot of nice clubs in Atlantic City. They were Black clubs, but they weren't segregated in the sense that they didn't allow Whites. Anybody could come; if you had green, that was always the answer." And an increasing number of Black people in Atlantic City, despite the limitations and harassment they confronted, did in fact have the green.

ATLANTIC CITY TO YEADON EXPRESS

According to Woodruff Brooks, by the late 1950s, Atlantic City's Black population had created a "stable middle class" that included doctors, educators and lawyers who owned their own homes. The environment proved to be an attractive one for young entrepreneurs such as Carson Puriefoy. In time, his business interests in Atlantic City contributed to a heightened cultural status for the Nile Swim Club. They offered access to the iconic performers who regularly appeared in the Black clubs on Kentucky

Harry Belafonte *(far right)* at the March on Washington, August 28, 1963. *Library of Congress.*

Avenue. For the Nile Swim Club's third annual achievement awards, held on December 1, 1961, at the Latin Casino in Merchantville, New Jersey, the legendary singer Harry Belafonte served as the guest of honor. According to a *Philadelphia Tribune* publicity piece, "a crowd of at least 900 persons, representing a complete sell-out, will witness the gala event."

The night of the event, Nancy L. Giddens reported for the *Philadelphia Tribune* that the "stars never shone brighter" than they did at the Nile Swim Club's "Night Out." Giddens described dinner as "elaborate and savory." This preceded club president Carson Puriefoy's presentation to Harry Belafonte of "an enormous plaque of gleaming bronze set against White mother of pearl on a mahogany base." Giddens observed, "There was no mistaking the pleasure enjoyed by Mr. Belafonte on receiving the Award. His handsome face was aglow." Following the award ceremony, the evening continued with "handsomely dressed guests dancing madly." And "as in all public gatherings these days," Giddens noted, "the Twist was king among the colorful crowd."

Denise Stewart Swann, daughter of Elmer Stewart, one of the Nile Swim Club's founders, recalls going to the Latin Casino with her parents. "As a young girl," she says, "my parents would let me go. They would take me with them." Every year, the Nile staged a fundraiser at the Latin Casino, and Stewart Swann cites the Temptations and other "big name groups" that performed. At times the artists also came by the Nile Swim Club of Yeadon, but Stewart Swann did not see them there. She says, "Those were adult only, at night, and children did not attend."

Four years after the Nile Swim Club hosted Belafonte, it feted Giddens with its Individual Achievement and Humanitarian Award. Giddens lived in

West Philadelphia and championed the Nile Swim Club as a member of the *Philadelphia Tribune*'s board of directors. In an article for the Urban History Association titled "Under Two Flags: How Nancy Giddens Built Bridges Between Black and Puerto Rican Neighbors," historian Alyssa Ribeiro chronicled how "through Nancy Giddens, a middle class African American woman, Puerto Ricans forged early ties with black communities."

Giddens leveraged a "strong and wide-ranging network of social connections" to support a variety of causes, including Heritage House, an educational and cultural institution for Black youth. Del Shields of WDAS-FM called Giddens "the woman who literally holds the key of influence and leadership among women in Philadelphia." To celebrate her work, on Friday, October 29, 1965, the Nile Swim Club welcomed the superstar singing group the Supremes to the Latin Casino. Little wonder that, as the *Philadelphia Tribune* cited, the club welcomed its "largest crowd ever, a standing room only audience."

That night, according to the *Tribune*, "the highways leading from Philadelphia and nearby areas were crowded with guests enroute" to the Nile's gala, one that also marked its seventh anniversary. The *Tribune* called the night a "thrilling success." The evening featured "dinner by candlelight and a sensational show sparked by The Supremes." During the award presentation, Giddens received "thunderous applause from an appreciative audience," which then went on to "enjoy ballroom dancing far into the wee hours."

The Place to See and Be Seen

Throughout the 1960s, the Nile Swim Club routinely made a splash welcoming well-known individuals to the pool and myriad social gatherings. This began at the pool's inception, which featured Clarence Peaks, a member of the 1960 National Football League champion Philadelphia Eagles. In opening the pool in 1959, as the *Philadelphia Tribune* reported, Peaks observed "with pride" the "work, perseverance and effort that today shows clearly the difference between good and great." Those who helped open the pool in other years include track stars Jesse Owens, John Thomas and Ira Davis. Such high-profile traffic through Yeadon prompted *Ebony* magazine to label it as Philadelphia's Black Main Line. At the center of it all, the Nile Swim Club became the place to "see and be seen."

In August 1964, *Ebony* ran a feature story on Patricia Evans, "Teen Age Beauty with Brains." At the age of seventeen, the senior honors student at Philadelphia's Overbrook High School won the Miss American Modeling Contest. She was the youngest competitor in a field of twenty-five contestants, and *Ebony* noted, "So enthusiastic was the audience's reaction that the judges had to warn it against breaking into loud and prolonged applause whenever she appeared on the runway." Evans remained unimpressed. She refused to "attach any significance to her modeling success" and remained focused on her studies at Overbrook.

At school, Evans served as her class president, belonged to the cheerleading squad and enjoyed swimming. *Ebony* wrote, "It was Pat's interest in swimming which resulted in her discovery by Tanya Maderas," the director of a Philadelphia modeling agency. Maderas "had been searching for attractive Negro teen-age models in hopes of cracking the color barrier at some of Philadelphia's dress houses and fashion salons."

Maderas found who she was looking for with Evans while spending a day at the Nile Swim Club. Maderas saw Evans "sitting on the diving board," and she "knew the moment I saw her, she was the girl I was looking for." She told *Ebony* that "Pat had the perfect face, figure and natural poise to make the grade." This resulted almost immediately in a photo of Evans in *Seventeen* magazine and an invitation to do a photo shoot in New York. Bill Mellix Jr. remembers it all well. Two others who frequented the Nile, both named Judy, also took part in the New York shoot. One, Judy Phillips, was Mellix Jr.'s girlfriend at the time, while the other, Judy Bell, later became his wife. As for Evans, the day served as the "springboard for her success," prompting Philadelphia mayor James H.J. Tate to award Patricia Evans with a "gold bracelet engraved with the Liberty Bell."

Maderas discovered Evans at the Nile's pool, but others found their own confidence by swimming there and by participating in the club's activities. Producer and screenwriter Marc Alexander told the *Philadelphia Inquirer* in 2012 that the Nile "was camp for us. We used to play basketball, sweat, dive into the pool, go home, eat dinner and come back and do the same thing." Longtime member Roosevelt Harper said, "This pool means everything. It's a sense of pride." He recalled that with three kids, "it hurt for me to pay the dues, but I knew I had to do it, even when I couldn't afford it."

Karen Hall Eskridge, a daughter of original members, adds that "there were six of us. For our parents to come up with the money to buy the bond… they were invested, they wanted to be a part of it, make it happen any way they could. They didn't want us to be disenfranchised." Lisa Nelson

Hayes, whose grandparents helped begin it all, added, "This is me. This is my history. This teaches us that we came from something and can do for ourselves." The Nile did precisely that for many, even if they did not realize it at the time. As Cleo Levetter, twelve years old, explained about the Swim Club to the *Philadelphia Inquirer*, "It's just a cool place to hang out."

Andrea Lee certainly thought so. Lee, a novelist whose *Russian Journal* (1981) earned a nomination for a National Book Award for nonfiction, fondly remembers her time at the Nile. In a 1982 op-ed for the *New York Times* titled "Black and Well-to-Do," Lee recounted asking her father, a Baptist minister and president of the Yeadon Civic Association, about the Swim Club's name. He "explained gravely: This is a club only for Egyptians." Lee added that she feels a "surge of well-being" when she returns "there in the summer to hear the symphony of lawn mowers and to find that the Nile Swim Club remains 'for Egyptians only.'" It also welcomed a certain "Fresh Prince."

From Yeadon to Bel Air

By the 1980s, splash parties constituted a long-standing tradition at the Nile. In August 1960, for example, the *Philadelphia Tribune* announced that the Swim Club planned "its most elaborate splash party since its grand opening." The night's entertainment included an "aquacade, swimming and diving exhibition and a fashion show." Open to all who purchased tickets, these became important fundraisers for the Nile and served to recruit new members. The club organized them around a popular Hawaiian theme. Denise Stewart Swann, daughter of one of the founders, Elmer Stewart, remembers these fondly. She recalls that for the kids, the night meant all hands on deck, or more aptly, in the pool. "The young girls, preteen, would do a water ballet show for the adults, while the boys contributed a diving exhibition."

"I used to do all that stuff," remembers Nile Swim Club president Anthony Patterson Sr., "for the Hawaiian Luau. We would dive and do a show." And what a show. Patterson says, "One time we had a high dive and a low dive. So, one guy would dive to one side, [and] we'd dive underneath each other. We would do one and a halves and back flips and all that stuff." He remembers the Johnson boys and Dupont as taking it all to the highest level. "They were the premier, the highlight of the show." Patterson laughs,

DJ Money B, aka Sam Patterson, maintains the Nile Swim Club's tradition of outstanding DJs. *Anthony Patterson Sr.*

"I was kind of in the middle, the opening act. Then the guys who could do the two and a halves came up." For the grand finale, Patterson says, "We would close with some flips and cannonballs and some figure fours. We'd splash the water everywhere. It was a pretty good show," Patterson recalls. "I enjoyed doing that."

In 1961, the *Tribune* reported, "Throngs of spectators adorned the already colorful grounds and enjoyed an aquatic show, dancing and dinner." Original club member Doris Fuller Moody remembers, "I would round up every friend I had. Sometimes I had five or six tables, and people were so happy to be there." The Nile Swim Club transcended swimming to become, according to Karen Hall Eskridge, an important "social setting for our community." Stewart Swann says that once the pool opened for the summer,

"I lived over there, truly lived over there. My mother made me come home for lunch and dinner—that was usually under protest for me—but I would come home. But then I would go back over in the evening, and all of my friends were there."

That social setting attracted a young Fresh Prince in the early 1980s, before he departed for Bel Air. Ericka Rumi Grant recalls, "The first time Will Smith was there, he introduced himself as Fresh Prince with Jazzy Jeff." She adds, laughing, "But we already had our own DJ, Cash Money." Deborah Robinson Stewart concurs, as they saw Cash Money as the Nile's guy "because he grew up in the neighborhood. He's from Lansdowne." Grant says of the Fresh Prince's takeover of the club, "It was like offensive. Their equipment took up the whole pavilion, and they had their own little entourage. They came from Overbrook or wherever to Yeadon and thought they'd dominate what we had going on."

The Fresh Prince proceeded to win over the Nile's skeptics. Grant concedes that when "they started playing, we were like, okay. They can hop a little bit, scratch and mix." Only sixteen or so at the time, Grant and Robinson recognized that the Nile's new Fresh Prince and his partner "were really good. They were free stylin', and then later we heard it on the radio and we're like, 'That was the guy from the pool!' We decided he was able to stay." Lamont Ferrell remembers playing basketball with Smith and Jazzy Jeff on the Nile's court before the two set up. "It was great," he says. "And we had heard about them before; they had been doing things around town."

Ferrell recalls the performance as great and cites that soon after seeing them at the Nile, he saw them on television. "You're, like, the Fresh Prince of Bel Air? It's the same guy we saw at the Nile!" Today, of course, Ferrell adds about Will Smith, "He's a mega star." While the Fresh Prince and Jazzy Jeff moved on to garner larger audiences, the Nile Swim Club provided them with an early stage. The same held true for the Nile's own DJ Cash Money. He went on to work with artists such as Snoop Dogg and Public Enemy, while also becoming the first inductee into the DJ Hall of Fame.

THE PUSH FOR DOUBLE VICTORY

Uncle Sam Needs Nurses

The resounding early success achieved by the Nile Swim Club enabled it to expand three years after it opened. It purchased an additional two and a half acres in 1962. This provided the club, according to the *Philadelphia Tribune*, "a frontage of 600 feet along Union Avenue from Providence Road to Park Place." The new space allowed for adding "an outdoor theatre, two hand ball courts" and space for "volleyball, badminton and other games." The space also offered a chance to stage increasingly lavish events, which, in addition to providing entertainment, promoted social and political activism. In September 1962, the Nile organized a Jamaican Carnivale, held "in connection with the independence celebration of Jamaica as a member of the British Commonwealth of Nations."

On August 31, 1962, the *Philadelphia Tribune* reported that an "estimated 450 visiting guests, colorfully attired in Island dress" enjoyed a "tropical atmosphere" generated by "the beautiful pool dotted with lily plants…exotic flowers, bamboo poles and palm trees." Most impressive, the newspaper observed, "was the Match Lighting ceremony." It explained, "With all electric lights extinguished, all native Jamaicans struck a match, followed by lighted matches throughout the club as a record played the Jamaican National Anthem. The Jamaican flag was raised by Bruce Holland, a lifeguard. A citation to Jamaica was the solemn highlight of the evening."

For a some of the original members, their civic pride, their social activism and their perseverance to attain racial equality derived from their military service during the Second World War. During that conflict, the *Pittsburgh Courier*, America's most widely read African American newspaper, initiated a "Double Victory" campaign that called for the defeat of racism both abroad and at home. This resonated with the war's Black veterans. They first fought for the right to fight for their country. Then they returned home to continue the struggle for racial equality. Many resided in the Philadelphia area, including members of the famed Tuskegee Airmen, a pioneering group of African American aviators that consisted of pilots, mechanics, nurses, bombardiers and administrators.

In fact, Philadelphia contributed more pilots to the unit than any other American city except Chicago. These included Alfred "The Chief" Anderson and Roscoe "The Coach" Draper. Anderson famously got the program off the ground by taking First Lady Eleanor Roosevelt for a flight, at her request and, reportedly, to the chagrin of her aides. Draper, a student of Anderson's, trained most of the pilots. Despite its moniker, the Tuskegee Airmen also benefited from the contributions of women, including ones with ties to the Philadelphia area such as "Ms." Alma Elizabeth Bailey and Callie O. Gentry. Serving the unit as nurses, administrators and parachute riggers, the women confronted both racism and sexism before, during and after the war. The challenges proved exceptional.

Tuskegee Airmen Training. *Library of Congress.*

Consider the experience of Ms. Bailey. Born in Middlesboro, Kentucky, in 1925, a twin and one of seven children, Ms. Bailey grew up dreaming of a musical career. Her parents, both educated, provided lessons and support. So, too, did her Baptist church. Ms. Bailey became the lead singer in its choir. She yearned to one day sing opera professionally. That ended when America entered the Second World War in 1941. Ms. Bailey's mother advised, "Uncle Sam needs nurses, not opera singers." That proved true, but he required some convincing about the capabilities of Black nurses.

In 1943, the year Ms. Bailey graduated from high school, Congress passed the Nurse Training Act (the Bolton Act). This created the United States Cadet Nurse Corps (UNC), a nationwide program to send qualified young women to accredited nursing schools. It offered scholarships, but initially the applications only went to Middlesboro's White high school. This changed after a group of Black mothers learned of the scholarships and petitioned the local school superintendent for more information. He relented, and a window of opportunity opened. Ms. Bailey took advantage of this and received an award. She departed home to study nursing at the Tuskegee Institute in Tuskegee, Alabama.

Ms. Bailey joined dozens of other Black women to provide nursing care for the Tuskegee Airmen, a pioneering unit of African American aviators. In the process, they confronted near constant racism, even as they served a nation at war with fascists pursuing racist agendas overseas. Out of fear for their safety, officials insisted the nurses visit the nearby town of Tuskegee, predominantly White, only in large groups, during daylight and with a chaperone. Moreover, some of the nurses, including Ms. Bailey, unwittingly aided the Tuskegee Study of Untreated Syphilis in the African American, the inhumane secret government program. This effort monitored the progress of syphilis in untreated patients while resulting in suffering and further infection.

Ms. Bailey learned the truth about the program decades later when a whistleblower leaked its details. She immediately grasped the sexism that surfaced while caring for soldiers suffering from trauma in the psychiatric ward, where the primitive treatment included electrical shocks. Alone in the ward, populated by dozens of men damaged emotionally and mentally by the war, the nurses relied on security provided by guards. The men on duty obliged, provided the nurses agreed to date them. After Ms. Bailey refused to accept this condition, they abandoned their posts once she entered the wards. Defiantly, by using a letter opener she kept hidden in her blouse as a weapon, Ms. Bailey thwarted an attempted assault and rape.

The experiences of Ms. Bailey and the thousands of African American men and women who served in the Tuskegee Aviation program contributed to America's victory during the Second World War. This went largely unrecognized by White Americans for decades after the conflict's conclusion. So, too, did the efforts of other Black Americans to help win the war, whether as members of the Red Ball Express, the ones who kept General George Patton's tanks fueled, or as participants in the Battle of the Bulge fighting with the Blank Panthers tank unit. Black veterans remained undeterred from continuing the fight.

Red Lined

At the end of World War II, Philadelphia stood as America's third-largest city. Optimism ran high amid military demobilization and the lapsing of wartime rationing and restrictions. A building boom took place, and rows of small houses and garden apartments appeared in the city's sections of East Germantown, West Oak Lane and the Northeast. Philadelphia's colleges and universities grew markedly in enrollment due to the educational opportunities made possible for veterans under the GI Bill. The benefits of this legislation largely eluded America's Black veterans. The Veterans Administration encouraged African Americans to attend vocational schools. Of those who did receive funding for higher education, 95 percent went to HBCUs, long underfunded and now overwhelmed with large numbers of new students.

Black people also faced closed doors when attempting to utilize the GI Bill's housing benefits. In the Philadelphia area, suburbanization accelerated in the postwar years. With newly acquired housing and educational benefits, the families of White veterans began leaving urban spaces like Philadelphia for new housing developments that promised lower taxes, better schools and more green space. Levittown, Pennsylvania, a planned community located twenty-seven miles northeast of Philadelphia in Bucks County, became the model suburb. Built by Levitt and Sons in 1951, Levittown sprang up quickly. The builders utilized a new assembly line model that enabled fast construction, erecting more than seventeen thousand houses at a pace of one every sixteen minutes. The community offered plenty of amenities, including an Olympic-sized swimming pool, parks and playgrounds.

Daisy Myers holding one of her children. *Library of Congress.*

Levitt and Sons refused to sell homes to African Americans. Levittown remained White only until one owner independently sold a home to William and Daisy Myers, a Black couple, in 1957. They immediately faced racial harassment that became increasing violent. While the Federal Housing Authority, the American Civil Liberties Union and the National Association for the Advancement of Colored People opposed the discriminatory housing practices of Levitt and Sons, the company fought back. Moreover, redlining practices throughout the area continued to limit the housing opportunities available to the Philadelphia area's Black residents, military veterans and families.

For many then, especially Black veterans, the Nile Swim Club in the Black suburban enclave of Yeadon became part of what appeared to be an increasingly elusive "Double V" project. Karen Hall Eskridge's dad, an original member of the Nile Swim Club, moved to Yeadon from nearby Ardmore, Pennsylvania, where he grew up. A World War II veteran, he served with the Red Ball Express, working as a mechanic. A Purple Heart recipient, he lost part of his foot after stepping on a land mine. In his case, Hall Eskridge says, "I think he did utilize GI Bill benefits when they bought the house in Yeadon."

He moved there after the war with his wife, Hall Eskridge's mom. "They wanted the suburban life. Vets were coming home, and that's what was being touted at the time," Hall Eskridge says. Moreover, Yeadon offered a convenient place to live for his job, as he worked for the Pennsylvania Liquor Control Board, managing a nearby store. About the GI Bill, Hall

Eskridge observes, "There was a lot of discrimination; not everybody who was eligible received the benefits. But because he was wounded, it was maybe a little easier."

Community Cohesion

To purchase the land and build a facility in the late 1950s, Nile Swim Club founders went door to door, asking folks to join as original bond holders at a cost of $250. That equates to nearly $3,000 in 2023—no small sum of money. "Back in the day, 1958," observes Joseph William Harris, "you give somebody $250, you had to be convinced it was going someplace good." His dad, William, believed that it would. He became the seventy-eighth original member. Others who gave without hesitation included Eugene J. Richardson, a resident of Marion Lane in Philadelphia. He became the ninetieth member.

In total, there existed an initial 326 bond holders, 76 of whom resided in Yeadon, with contributions from others coming from people who lived in nearby communities such as Darby, Lansdowne, Glen Mills, Havertown and Chester. More than two dozen others, like Richardson, lived in Philadelphia. A veteran, Richardson earned his wings with the Tuskegee Airmen, but the war ended before he could deploy. Richardson likes to say about that, "It's why it stopped. Hitler heard I was coming over and killed himself."

Such a sense of humor likely contributed to Richardson's successful postwar career in education, first as a teacher and then as a principal. He served as a pioneer in racially integrating Philadelphia's public schools, volunteering to take a faculty position at a predominantly White school. While he experienced some resentment from other faculty, he received the support of the school district's administration. In terms of his students, he recalls, "They take you as you are."

Kenneth Earl Green, a former Nile Swim Club president and the son of one of its original members, recalls his dad's World War II experience. It included him being "thrown off a ship. He didn't know how to swim and he almost drowned." After his rescue, Green's father "vowed his kids would learn how to swim." After the war, when he moved to Yeadon and heard about the Nile Swim Club's call for members, "he was right in tune with it." During the war, Green's dad belonged to the Red Ball Express, a group of mostly Black soldiers tasked with trucking supplies to the front lines

Richard Allen (*center*) and other bishops of the AME Church. *Library of Congress.*

following the breakout of Allied forces from Normandy. Operating nearly six thousand vehicles for nearly three months in 1944, the Red Ball Express delivered 12,500 tons per day. This often transpired while taking heavy fire from enemy forces.

Joseph William Harris's dad also drove for the Red Ball Express. He told Harris and his brother of driving through wartime France at night with his vehicle's lights turned off as he came under fire. After the war, Harris's dad founded a successful trucking company and became an early supporter of the Nile Swim Club. He additionally assumed a role in the civil rights movement, becoming "Dr. Martin Luther King Jr.'s bodyguard when he came to Philadelphia."

In addition, as Harris remembers, "My father gave King a flatbed truck to use as a stage for his speech in West Philadelphia, near 40th Street." Meanwhile, Jacquelynn Puriefoy recollects that during her childhood, Paul Robeson, a Harlem Renaissance figure and civil rights activist investigated during the McCarthy era in a misguided effort to link civil rights and Communism, "used to have dinner at our house," Jacquelynn laughs. "But I didn't know who he was." In the case of Yvonne Burnley Studevan, her family connects back to Richard Allen, the founder of the African Methodist Episcopal Church (AME). Established in 1794 in Philadelphia, the AME Church is the first independent Black denomination in America.

Allen, the first bishop elected in the AME Church, presided over an 1830 meeting convened in Philadelphia and attended by the nation's Black leaders. Historians credit it as beginning the Negro Convention Movement, an important component of Black institution building in the United States.

Burnley Studevan says, "I'm seventh generation, so it makes him my great-great-great-grandfather." Burnley Studevan's dad served in the Second World War in the U.S. Navy and began working at the Philadelphia Naval Yard after the war. Through her family's history, the commitment to a "Double Victory" runs deeps. She adds, "We've had somebody in our family who has served in every war from the American Revolution."

NOT ABOUT HATE

This intersection of past and present, the willingness to persevere and the commitment to equality made a profound impact on the children of the original members. John H. "Sonny" Sanford grew up on Fairview Avenue and graduated as valedictorian of Yeadon High School. He graduated with a degree in political science from Penn State University in 1961. When he returned home from State College for the summer, he worked as a lifeguard at the Nile Swim Club. His father, Cecil, an original member, became the ninety-second bondholder. He spoke to the *Philadelphia Tribune* in 1984 about his son, saying that "I wanted my son to be an engineer, but I later found that he was determined to make it in his field, when he graduated at the top of his college class of 200."

That determination led "Sonny" Sanford to a distinguished career as an aviator in the U.S. Army. After overseas tours in Germany, Korea and Vietnam, Sanford rose to the rank of general and served as the executive secretary of the Department of Defense. His military decorations included the Army Commendation Medal with three Oak Leaf Clusters, the Bronze Star with three Oak Leaf Clusters, the Air Medal with thirteen Oak Leaf Clusters, the Distinguished Flying Cross and the Legion of Merit. In 1984, General Stanford became the 22nd Military Traffic Management Commander of the Western area. Following his military career, in 1995, Sanford became the first Black superintendent of the Seattle, Washington public school system.

The spirit of the long struggle to achieve civil rights imbued the Swim Club's origins and shaped its culture. Harris fondly remembers Thomas Gary, one who worked for the quartermaster on military purchasing and who initially acted as the Nile's membership chairman. "Good with numbers," as Harris cites, Gary proved instrumental in "organizing the foundation of the Swim Club." Harris recollects the efforts of Gary and other original members such as "Mr. [Elmer] Stewart and Mr. [Booker] Brown to make the pool something special. Not in bringing up any hate or anything," because others excluded them. "Nah, they said we'll just build our own. And that's what they did. That takes hutzpah."

Indeed, it did. So did their commitment to equality. One month after the pool opened in 1959, the *Philadelphia Tribune* noted that "even though the pool's membership is largely Negro from the west end of Yeadon (and its environs) its charter and practice do not deny anyone admission because of color, race or creed." It continued to stress, "Even though this open-door policy has been shared by a few, the club wants it to be known to all that its doors are open democratically in every sense of the word." The paper cited that "[m]any have said that the Nile Swim Club has brought more neighbors together than any project participated in before."

The Nile continued to bring neighbors together, not only to swim but also to participate in the push for civil rights, nationally and internationally. On August 28, 1963, civil rights leaders A. Phillip Randolph and Bayard Rustin, a native of West Chester, Pennsylvania, located nineteen miles west of Yeadon, orchestrated one of the largest rallies for human rights in American history. A group of 250,000 people, predominantly African American, convened in Washington, D.C., to stage the March on Washington for Jobs and Freedom. Dr. Martin Luther King Jr. offered the last words of the day, delivering his "I Have a Dream" speech from in front of the Lincoln Memorial. Historians credit the day with provoking the passage of the Civil Rights Act of 1964.

More than one thousand members of the Nile attended the March on Washington. Swim Club president Byron Reed organized the trip, which, according to the *Philadelphia Tribune*, constituted "the largest affair ever held by the Nile." That certainly appeared to be the case to Barbara Ann Johnson Williams, daughter of founding member Dr. William H. Johnson. She showed up at the pool that day and found, to her surprise, nobody there. Everybody had gone to Washington. Much to her chagrin, Johnson Williams did not know about the march. A college student, she had just returned from a study abroad, which disconnected her from developments back home. She jokes, "I thought the Beatles were bugs. I couldn't understand the excitement."

Forging the Nile

Barbara Ann Johnson Williams says that her dad came to Philadelphia from Virginia, where racist laws prevented him, a physician, from providing appropriate care to his pregnant wife. He brought her to Mercy-Douglass, located on Woodlawn Avenue in West Philadelphia, to give birth. As Jessica Markey Locklear from Temple University's Special Collection wrote, the doctors and nurses trained at Mercy-Douglass played "an instrumental role in the desegregation of health care in Pennsylvania."

In Philadelphia, Dr. Johnson opened a practice at 52nd and Race Streets and moved his young family to 97 Fairview Avenue in Lansdowne, Pennsylvania, a town adjacent to West Yeadon. There he sought to join the Lansdowne Swim Club and received back his uncashed check. Johnson Williams learned later that this resulted, in part, from the machinations of her best friend's father, who "wanted to keep it White." She remembers that "sometime after that, Elmer Stewart approached him about creating a club and they then convened a meeting at my father's house." According to Dr. Johnson's *Memoirs of an Eastern Shore Physician* (2002), the ones in attendance included Booker Brown, Thomas Gary, Byron Reed, Robert and Zoe Mask, Elmer Stewart, Carson Puriefoy and, of course, Dr. Johnson.

Of that group, Zoe Mask assumed a prominent role. According to Rachel Athelia Anderson's article for the *Philadelphia Inquirer* commemorating the Nile Swim Club's thirtieth anniversary, in the spring of 1957, tired of watching their young daughter "sweat and grow restless in the heat of summer," Zoe Mask "rushed to put in an application" to join the newly announced Yeadon Swim Club. After ten days, the Masks continued to wait for a response. As Zoe Mask grew more anxious, her husband advised not to jump to conclusions but rather to "wait and see what happens." After more waiting, nothing happened. Zoe Mask then wrote to borough officials, explaining that "she would appreciate a written letter of acceptance or denial."

This prompted a call from a borough official a few days later. Robert Mask remembered that the official "never really gave them a straight answer." Whatever he said, or did not say, it left the Masks convinced that "they were being excluded from the Yeadon Swim Club because of their race." The Masks began rallying other Black families in Yeadon "for a showdown with the Borough Council." Little consensus existed about how best to proceed when they arrived to meet the others at Dr. Johnson's home in November 1957, as the Masks told the *Philadelphia Inquirer*. While there, according to Robert Mask, "My wife decided not to fight," proposing instead, "We'll just show them that we can do the same thing." So they did.

That winter, they organized an endeavor that resulted in fifty members. At that point, the group realized that it needed "a formal name for the

First officers of the Nile Swim Club of Yeadon. *From left*: Carson Puriefoy, president; Zoe Mask, secretary; and Elmer Stewart, vice-president. *Nile Swim Club of Yeadon historical documents.*

pool, although it had not yet been built." One soon came from Zoe Mask, who suggested "the name Nile thinking that it would conjure up exotic images of Egypt Africa, the motherland." This worked. As "Prejudice and Pride…The Story of the Nile" explains, the name sought "to harken back to the ancient, life-giving waters at the heart and soul of African American heritage."

The name proved easy to identify, as did the architect. The newly named Nile Swim Club of Yeadon formed a nonprofit corporation in February 1958 and contracted Harold Boyd, a young Black architect, to design the club. According to "Prejudice and Pride," the "Nile Swim Club could not possibly be as lavish as the White club turned out to be." Boyd, newly awarded his degree, "moved forward with pride and enthusiasm," and with a plan "simple and more utilitarian in design." From "that very simplicity and utility sprung equality itself." Assuming, of course, the new nonprofit could raise the funds necessary to render the design a reality.

I'll Believe It When I See It

The Nile Swim Club's Articles of Incorporation state that the corporation's purpose was to "provide for the health, welfare, culture and recreation of its members through the ownership, construction, operation and maintenance of a swimming pool and other facilities and that this is a corporation which does not contemplate pecuniary gain or profit." It lists as the incorporators Carson Puriefoy; Elmer Stewart; Zoe Lorraine Mask; Virginia F. Shipley; Robert W. Mask; W.H. Henderson, MD; George O. Barnes; Booker Brown; William F. Brown; Elmer Cochrane; Earl Fisher, MD; Gladys S. Frazier; Sarah E. Gibson; W.H. Johnson, MD; Nathaniel C. Kimbrough; William Green; Ada G. McConnell; Lee McNeill; William Mellix Jr.; Plummer Morton; Mabel C. Motley; Harry Porter; Byron F. Reed; Jerome Robinson; and David Young.

All the incorporators lived in Yeadon except for Lansdowne resident W.H. Johnson. The club's officers included Carson Puriefoy, president; Elmer Stewart, vice-president; Zoe Lorraine Mask, recording secretary; Virginia F. Shipley, corresponding secretary; Robert W. Mask, financial secretary; and W.H. Henderson, treasurer. Organized on a non-stock basis, the corporation's assets, cited by the articles, equaled "none." On September 26, 1958, Judge Henry G. Sweney, presiding over the Court of Common Pleas of Delaware County, gave the Nile Swim Club's Articles of Incorporation his stamp of approval.

The Nile Swim Club's incorporators numbered twenty-five and included three physicians. In 1989, Robert Mask recounted to the *Philadelphia Inquirer*, "There were other people interested, but they didn't want to put up their money without seeing water in the pool." This constituted a dilemma. The Nile Swim Club needed money to build a pool. According to club by-laws, the incorporators received charge to "seek loans from friends and neighbors in the community." The club set up the loans as "non-negotiable, non-assessable, non-transferrable, non-profit-sharing and non-interest bearing," with a fifty-year date of maturity.

Potential donors proved unwilling to invest in a pool planned and not built. The prevailing mantra, recalls Jacquelynn Puriefoy-Brinkley, played to the refrain, "I'll believe it when I see the water in the pool. That's what a lot of people said." The situation prompted the Nile's organizers to visit the Girard Bank branch in Upper Darby, Pennsylvania, an adjacent town to Yeadon, to explain the problem. The bank responded with a solution. It offered members the chance to take out twelve-month loans. Problem solved—almost.

Puriefoy-Brinkley remembers "disagreements about the Nile between my mother and father." She continues, "And I think," laughing, "that my father paid the money for the original land. I think that's how he got to be president." Still giggling, she points out that on the document from the State of Pennsylvania affirming that "the name of the corporation is the Nile Swim Club of Yeadon and that the said name has been registered with the Department of State," the club's listed address, 210 Providence Road, Yeadon, Pennsylvania, "is the same as my family's house." Puriefoy-Brinkley says that when she saw the document for the first time, "That's what it was all about, and that's the kind of thing my father would've done. And, of course, I know everybody paid him back."

That proved to be a good thing, as the Nile Swim Club purchased two acres in September 1958. Puriefoy-Brinkley says, "The borough was very happy to sell them the land so they wouldn't bother them about the other swim club." Richard Barnes, an original club member, knew the area well. "It used to be our playground," Barnes recalls, littered with old fifty-five-gallon drums and wooden pallets. Barnes and his childhood friends labeled their stomping grounds "Radiation Park." This constituted the Sullivan tract, a dump site for local chemical companies. When work began to transform the site into a swim club, Barnes could not contain his curiosity. He went exploring, climbing down into the newly dug hole in the ground made for the pool. A downpour resulted in a muddy mess that rendered Barnes stuck in the muck. "They had to come find me," Barnes laughs, "my sister or the fire department or somebody." The makeshift posse rescued him, but according to Barnes, "My shoes are still down there."

Lost shoes seemed a small price to pay on July 11, 1959, when the pool officially opened. Puriefoy-Brinkley "remembers standing there at that gate with my father looking at the water, and I saw the tears coming down.

I'll never forget that, never." The day proved a memorable one for many. Malcolm Poindexter, an Emmy Award–winning journalist and a 1996 inductee into the Philadelphia Broadcast Pioneers Hall of Fame, witnessed it as a reporter for the *Philadelphia Tribune*. As a Black reporter assigned to cover both the Democratic and the Republican National Conventions, not long before, in 1948, Poindexter conducted interviews in the hall. Officials at neither meeting allowed Black journalists on the convention floor.

The Pool

The Nile Swim Club's opening resonated deeply with Poindexter as he grasped its historical significance. He watched the scene and recorded it in wonder. Poindexter wrote that "more that 700 adults and youngsters gathered to marvel at the $75,000.00 project begun last April. Excellent weather preceding a late evening downpour favored the twice-postponed opening." Remarkably, the Nile Swim Club went from idea to execution in about eighteen months. Puriefoy-Brinkley, even as a teen, grasped the day's importance. She says, "A lot of people thought it wouldn't [happen], a lot of people. But it did."

Elmer Stewart's daughter, Denise Stewart Swann, a child at the time, posed with a shovel at the club's groundbreaking. She cites the day fondly, one she remembers "so clear. I helped lay the sod for the grass that we used for the pool." After that, her ties to the pool never diminished. She took her first job there, working at the snack counter. She became a lifeguard and then "graduated to the front desk," where she fondly remembers working many years. On July 4, 1968, Stewart Swann received the Miss NAACP crown at the Swim Club from the Darby-area NAACP.

Once Stewart Swann became a teacher at Yeadon High and started a family of her own, the Nile remained central to her and her family's life. The club provided swimming instruction and a safe space for her children. While they grew up, once again, Stewart Swann says, "I was there every day, watching my kids learn how to swim." Even after she moved with her family to Maryland, her heart remained at the Nile. Stewart Swann says, "I continue to keep my membership up because I know this was my parents' dream." This kind of commitment to the pool is common. Lisa Ivery also moved to Maryland for a time and says, "I kept my membership so I could swim when I came home." She adds, "I think I got that from my mom. She

Groundbreaking for the Nile Swim Club of Yeadon. *Nile Swim Club of Yeadon historical documents.*

used to say, regardless of what we are doing or how often we get there, we're paying our dues."

Mark Miller is the son of a former Nile board president. His family, number seventy-nine on the original bond holder list, remains active at the pool. His mother, Lauretta, serves on the senior committee, orchestrating activities such as the Senior Line Dancing, while also helping fundraise. Mark says, "Here we are sixty-three years later and still active. The 'pool,' as we call it, has really shaped us as a family and as individuals." He says, "My wife, from Pittsburgh, tells me that when you say 'the pool,' it's with such inflection, such reverence." His brother Norman says that feeling is widespread. "I live in South Florida now, meet people down here who know and love the Nile." Of the Nile's community, Lisa Ivery says, "There are lots of people I met at the pool, then went with to high school. We are still in touch. It's just an indescribable feeling."

A Good Deal

At the club's dedication in July 1959, when Stewart Swann's parents and the others finally realized their dream, Zoe Mask cut a ribbon leading to the pool. Poindexter reported, "Her command to swim touched off a bit of unofficial dunking by members of the club." Those feeling the fruits of their efforts were, in order of fully clothed dunking, Thomas Gary; Carson Puriefoy, president; Elmer Stewart; Mrs. Mask; Byron Reed; Dr. Howard Henderson; William Mellix Jr.; Joseph McNeal, attorney; and Booker Brown. According to Poindexter, "Stewart earlier cited the support of three of the founders' wives, Madams Florence Stewart, Zoe L. Mask and Louise Gary. Each was presented a gift."

Poindexter identified other program participants as the Color Guard of Post 974, Darby, led by Willie G. Childs; Dolores Wilson; Reverend I.N. Patterson III, pastor of Bethel AME Church, Lansdowne; Mrs. Audrey Brodie; Howard Carrington; and Reverend Arthur Adkins, DD, pastor of Mount Sinai Baptist Church, Lansdowne. The gathering testified to the community's support for the newly opened Swim Club. What they saw surely did not disappoint. For the founders, the opening constituted a milestone, one they had worked tirelessly to attain. It proved satisfying. Carson Puriefoy remarked, "I have gained more than I have given."

Poindexter learned from Thomas Gary that the main pool measured seventy-five feet by thirty-five feet and featured a twelve-foot-deep diving well that measured thirty feet by thirty feet. Plans at the time called for installation of one-meter and three-meter diving boards. A wading pool for children complemented the main pool. Poindexter explained, "The pool base is of Granite, a process for which concrete is blown under pressure. It has a marble and tile rim." He called the Swim Club's site "attractive" and noted, "Inside the bath house are a snack bar, manager's office and locker room." Poindexter added, "Money for construction was raised through the sale of bonds and a bank loan. Membership has attracted persons throughout the Delaware Valley area."

Jet magazine, also there to witness the grand opening, reported, "The club sits back from a street in Yeadon and in the rear is a grove of trees that makes the city seem miles away. On another fronting stand new ranch-style homes owned by Negroes, many of them members of the club. The club presently owns two and one-quarter acres of land. The pool is an L-shaped beauty, 3½ to 5½ to 12 feet deep and at its greatest length is 75 feet long. Two diving boards, one high and one low, are erected at the deep end to challenge divers and accomplished swimmers."

Nile receptionists Deborah Barnes and Folasayo Aiyebo. *Author's collection.*

Cliff "Brother" Brock loves the Nile. *Jacqueline Pochadt, Nile Swim Club of Yeadon Collection.*

Left: Nile Swim Club treasurer Deborah Barnes and president Anthony Patterson Sr.. *Cheri Carter.*

Below: Welcome to the Nile. *Author's collection.*

Swim Club leaders "Love the Nile." *Jacqueline Pochadt, Nile Swim Club of Yeadon Collection.*

Shooting hoops at the Nile. *Jacqueline Pochadt, Nile Swim Club of Yeadon.*

Dancing on the Nile. *Jacqueline Pochadt, Nile Swim Club of Yeadon Collection.*

From left: Gabriel Johnson (lifeguard), with correspondence secretary Latifah Fields, lifeguard Levon Stewart, Nile president Anthony Patterson Sr. and lifeguards Drew Dunham-Snipes and Sa'ood Gibson. *Cheri Carter.*

"Glow Party" at the Nile. *Jacqueline Pochadt, Nile Swim Club of Yeadon Collection.*

"Glow Party" smile. *Jacqueline Pochadt, Nile Swim Club of Yeadon Collection.*

Anna Bullock, "Lil Mis Juneteenth PA 2023." *Jacqueline Pochadt, Nile Swim Club of Yeadon Collection.*

Mile High Diving at the Nile. *Jacqueline Pochadt, Nile Swim Club of Yeadon Collection.*

Snack time. *Jacqueline Pochadt, Nile Swim Club of Yeadon Collection.*

Water babies. *Jacqueline Pochadt, Nile Swim Club of Yeadon Collection.*

Water aerobics. *Jacqueline Pochadt, Nile Swim Club of Yeadon Collection.*

Grooving by the Nile. *Jacqueline Pochadt, Nile Swim Club of Yeadon Collection.*

Splash party. *Jacqueline Pochadt, Nile Swim Club of Yeadon Collection.*

Nile board members (left to right) Jessica Pointer, Clifford Brock, Frank Brown and Amorette Mason. *Jacqueline Pochadt, Nile Swim Club of Yeadon Collection.*

Junteeenth. *From left*: Lori Patterson, Jaye Patterson, Jordyn Patterson, Julianna Patterson, Aaliyah Patterson and Ruth Patterson Presley. *Jacqueline Pochadt, Nile Swim Club of Yeadon Collection.*

Testing the waters. *Jacqueline Pochadt, Nile Swim Club of Yeadon Collection.*

Above: Jessie's Garden. *Jacqueline Pochadt, Nile Swim Club of Yeadon Collection.*

Left: Tree planting. *Jacqueline Pochadt, Nile Swim Club of Yeadon Collection.*

Above: Picnic on the Nile. *Jacqueline Pochadt, Nile Swim Club of Yeadon Collection.*

Left: Barbecue, with Ramondo Frank and Anthony Patterson Sr. *Jacqueline Pochadt, Nile Swim Club of Yeadon Collection.*

Above: Nile style. *Jacqueline Pochadt, Nile Swim Club of Yeadon Collection.*

Right: Anthony Patterson Sr., Lori Patterson, Julia Hill and Amier Boyce. *Jacqueline Pochadt, Nile Swim Club of Yeadon Collection.*

Board member Andre Andrews providing free swim lessons. *Jacqueline Pochadt, Nile Swim Club of Yeadon Collection.*

Swim paddle pro. *Jacqueline Pochadt, Nile Swim Club of Yeadon Collection.*

Big Nile smile. *Jacqueline Pochadt, Nile Swim Club of Yeadon Collection.*

Independence. *Jacqueline Pochadt, Nile Swim Club of Yeadon Collection.*

The Nile Swim Club Board. *Jacqueline Pochadt, Nile Swim Club of Yeadon Collection.*

Swim. Eat. Chill. Repeat. *Jacqueline Pochadt, Nile Swim Club of Yeadon Collection.*

OPENING DAY CELEBRATION - JULY 11, 1959

(L. to R.) Carson Puriefoy, Pres.; Elmer Stewart, Vice-Pres.; Dr. W. H. Henderson, Treasurer; Byron F. Reed, Program-Publicity Chairman; Robert Mask, Financial Secretary; Mrs. Zoe Mask, Recording Secretary; Thomas Gary, Membership Chairman.

Shortly after this picture was taken, the above officers and committee chairmen were 'dunked' in traditional fashion after the ribbon cutting ceremony.

Nile Swim Club of Yeadon opening program booklet. *Nile Swim Club of Yeadon historical documents.*

CERTIFICATE OF LOAN

No. 3 $250.00

The Nile Swim Club

INCORPORATED UNDER THE LAWS OF THE STATE OF PENNSYLVANIA

A non-profit corporation

YEADON, PA.

This is to certify that

Carson Puriefoy

has loaned THE NILE SWIM CLUB $250.00. This certificate is non-negotiable, non-assessable, non-transferable, non-profit-sharing, non-interest-bearing, and is otherwise subject to the Provisions and limitations of the Bylaws of the Club.

IN WITNESS WHEREOF, the said Corporation has caused this Certificate to be signed by its duly authorized officers and its Corporate Seal to be hereunto affixed this seventeenth *day of* July *A. D. 19*57.

Carson Puriefoy
SECRETARY
President

Zoe [illegible]
PRESIDENT
Secretary

Carson Puriefoy's original Nile Swim Club of Yeadon certificate. *Nile Swim Club of Yeadon historical documents.*

Once open, the Swim Club became the hub of West Yeadon. In turn, West Yeadon became a destination, especially for the region's African American population. Doris Fuller Moody, an original member from West Philadelphia, says that transpired because "we would tell our friends about it." She remembers when they opened the club, "somebody sent Byron Reed [Nile publicity committee] to talk to me and my husband." Reed informed them that the Nile constituted the "only solely Negro owned swim club in the city." Fuller Moody and her husband, a World War II veteran, only replied by asking, "How much?" In their minds, "If you could afford it, or if you could afford the sacrifice," no option existed otherwise except to join the Nile Swim Club. *Jet* magazine agreed, calling "$250.00 for a life membership a good deal."

Getting Acclimated

As a child, Fuller Moody swam at a city pool in West Philadelphia, a ten-block walk from her house. It was segregated by gender, alternating days for males and females. This existed as common practice for city pools at the time, which operated under overcrowded and understaffed conditions. This caused parents to worry about their children drowning, as no opportunities existed to learn how to swim. Like other kids in West Philly, Fuller Moody and her sisters frequented the pool without her mother's knowledge. Her mother, house bound, did not like them visiting the city pool unsupervised, but there existed no other place for them to go. As *Jet* magazine commented about private pools at the time, "Negroes are not usually admitted to membership."

This situated the Nile Swim Club, for Fuller Moody and other initial members, as a welcome oasis, a chance of "getting our children acclimated to the water." The pool's lifeguards proved up to the task. Andrew Kenneth Andrews grew up in southwest Philadelphia and graduated from Bartram High School. Andrews recalls it as a "nice little hike" from his neighborhood to Yeadon, but he heard from his friend Waverly Martin that "they had this pool and I wanted to see it. I was a swimmer." Andrews learned how to swim at the Sherwood pool, a city pool located at 56th and Christian Streets in West Philadelphia, now part of the Christy Recreation Center. Andrews remembers his time there fondly. "There was a seventy-foot pool there." He clarifies, "[It] wasn't no little pool."

At Sherwood, Andrews learned to swim from Preston Barnes, "one of the top Philadelphia swimmers, and he went to West Philadelphia High School." Barnes, along with others whom Andrews remembers by their nicknames "Baby" and "Bubbles," mentored Andrews. He reflects, "These guys were real good, and they weren't really teachers; we were all just coming up together. They taught me how to swim at a young age, and these guys were swimmers. And that's very rare to find these kinds of Black swimmers right in your neighborhood. They were the tops at West Philly. They still got pictures of these guys, that's how good they were." Andrews loved the water and proved an exemplary student. On the Bartram High School Swim team, Andrews broke the city record in the backstroke.

Andrews made his way to the Nile Swim Club in the 1980s. When he saw the Nile pool for the first time, he thought it was "beautiful." He marveled, "It had two double-deck diving boards, and what really blew me out of the water, I thought it was a White pool. It wasn't. It was a Black pool." He laughs, "Say what? Come on!" Hoping to become a lifeguard, "Mr. June" asked Andrews if he knew how to swim. With his certifications, Andrews found the question funny, but he recalls, "That was the beginning of me at the Nile Swim Club." A labor safety coordinator for AMTRAK, Andrews loved to teach swimming, especially to "inner city kids." In addition to lifeguarding at the Nile's pool, he did the same at the YMCA. He felt stifled at the YMCA, though, thinking that "they never gave me enough time with the kids." It worked differently at the Nile, according to Andrews. "They let me do my thing."

From the onset, the Swim Club opened its door to Philadelphia's kids to let them also do their thing. Back in the early 1960s, Yvonne Burnley Studevan says, "This is going to sound crazy, but this is what I'd do." It involved a weekly bathroom ritual. She remembers Sunday morning trips there "because I could see into the parking lot of the pool." That mattered because "on Sundays the bus would come to bring kids from West Philadelphia to the Swim Club." She watched and listened. At the first sign the bus approached, she "would beeline down the steps, bathing suit and stuff ready." She anticipated seeing her church friends from Philadelphia. They would meet in the locker room and talk "about the boys that were going to be there." She recalls, "We knew exactly where they were going to go at the pool. They'd be strutting in front of us, and we would be lounging in the chairs checking them out. We would all sit in those chairs and decide how we were going to pose."

But Burnley Studevan went to the Nile for reasons other than to pose for boys. She says, "I won my first swimming trophy there!" During one of its annual Fourth of July races, Burnley Studevan, then thirteen or fourteen years old, remembers "jumping into the pool and getting to the end before half the other people made it halfway across." This despite a "wardrobe malfunction." She says, "I was really skinny, and my mother would find me these cute little stitched one-piece bathing suits. Well, y'know how you throw your arms back to do a racing dive? I pulled my arms forward, and the stitches broke." That all resulted in her bathing suit getting pushed down to around her waist. She realized her "bathing suit was down but was trying to win a race, pulling the suit up and swimming at the same time." She laughs, "Good thing I was flat chested."

Deborah Robinson Stewart does not remember when she learned how to swim. She remembers, "We would just watch the older kids and model after them." She continues, "We always wanted to emulate the older kids who were in the deep end. They used to always play a game called 'Fox in the Hole,' and we wanted to join in. But they kept telling us that we were too young. We couldn't wait to get older." The game, Robinson Stewart explains, featured one person treading water in the deep end. The goal "was to get past them without getting tagged, so you really had to know how to swim because to do that you needed to go down deep, and on that side it is eleven feet."

Wanda Reese started to frequent the pool daily while in the fourth or fifth grade. She lived in a multi-generation house and recalls that "one day my great uncle said to me, okay, I got you a membership." Reese remembers "being so excited. None of my parents or relatives ever went with me. I just went across the street, could go by myself." Such a short distance, and on most days, she could not cross it fast enough. She says, "I remember sitting on the steps some days just waiting for the pool to open because I could not wait to go swimming, then I'd swim all day." She had plenty of company. She recollects, "Most of us were there all day, supervised only by the lifeguards and pool staff."

The Nile enabled parents to trust the club, its members and its staff to teach their kids how to swim and, just as importantly, to develop a sense of community. Fuller Moody remembers, "We could leave our children, and they learned to swim while they were just walking. I think about those days, and I can't believe...but there it is, it is still there." In those days, Fuller Moody and other parents volunteered to be there when they could. "Ms." Alma Elizabeth Bailey offers, "It was like a voluntary cooperation group. Look out for each other, one another's children; we were so happy to have the Nile." Fuller Moody adds, "We wanted our children to be in a safe place and learn how to swim." And on their behalf, as Lisa Ivery attests, "I didn't want to be anywhere else but the pool. Even if it was raining, I wanted to be there."

The Nile Swim Club became those things and much more. *Jet* magazine raved about the club's facilities. "The clubhouse," it observed, "painted a warm pink, houses the office, snack bar, men's and women's rest rooms and showers with additional large rooms for keeping clothing of members and guests." The poolside featured a jukebox that played "cool music" and served to "lend a festive mood augmented by gaily colored pennants and other nautical regalia." With a tennis court, picnic area and "swings for the kiddies," *Jet* suggested that "families can spend the day at the club picnicking, swimming, sunning, dancing and in general building good social relations." It asserted that "the pool keeps the youngsters busy and acts as a deterrent to delinquency." Lisa Ivery remembers, "The parents at the club had a great time, they could all get together and enjoy themselves." She adds, for the kids, "It was like every parent was your parent. Nobody was letting anybody's kids do what they weren't supposed to be doing."

Even with such supervision, however, for the kids who went to the pool daily, there was no place else they wished to be. Jacquelynn Puriefoy-Brinkley says, "I used to sleep in my bathing suit. And in the morning, when I heard the music—we had a jukebox—I'd roll out of bed, and I'd stay the whole day, every day, at the pool." This experience represented a common one. Lisa Ivery remembers that if family errands existed in the morning, she hopped in the car prepared, packing her suit and everything else, to be dropped at the pool when it opened. "Growing up," she told the *Philadelphia Inquirer*, "it was the place that everybody wanted to be." Norman Miller adds, "We were the tail end of the baby boom, and West Yeadon was just filled with kids. Hundreds of us. And we were all at the pool every day. I can tell you that those of us that experienced the Nile in the 1960s and 1970s, we're still close."

HIGH-WATER MARK

Pooling Together

Deborah Robinson Stewart and Ericka Rumi Grant, best friends since third grade, say that they "pooled together every day, every summer. It was like a big family; our whole neighborhood went there." The *Philadelphia Tribune* observed in 1964, "When the Nile opens its doors for the summer it is like taking the summer acquaintances out of storage." Robinson Stewart adds, "We just knew everybody there. We always had fun; there was always so much going on. It was very much a community. It was a safe space." That, of course, is what the Nile Swim Club founders set out to create. They did so through meticulous organization and an insistence on maintaining the highest of standards.

The Nile Swim Club's members adopted by-laws on June 13, 1959. The club's "purposes and objectives" were "to promote and provide, to the extent possible, for the moral, educational, physical and social well-being of its members." To do these things, the by-laws made explicit the club's family-friendly environment. They note that the club "shall not engage in the sale or handling of alcoholic liquors, malt beverages or other intoxicants." Moreover, they stipulate that "the bringing of alcoholic liquors, malt beverages or other intoxicants on the premises or property of the Corporation is strictly prohibited, whether by Officers, employees, members or their guests." They banned "anyone from the premises," in fact, who appeared to be in "an intoxicated condition."

Unlike other area swim clubs, such as the ones in Lansdowne and Yeadon, the Nile Swim Club opened its application process to everybody, refusing to discriminate according to race or ethnicity. It did limit its overall membership to 375 members, and as it was a private swim club, the by-laws clarified that "[f]amilies desiring to become members in the Nile Swim Club of Yeadon must be approved by the Board of Governors." The by-laws further established different types of memberships: "A," "B" and "C." Only the first 275 elected became "A" members, ones with equity in the Swim Club.

"B" members, according to the by-laws, "shall be those elected for permanent membership to replace any retiring Class 'A' members, or, at the discretion of the Board, may be elected to bring the membership to its full quota." Type "C" members, or associate members, depended on board discretion in replacing any types "A" or "B" members who became "temporarily inactive." Type "C" membership was afforded no voting rights and expired at the end of "the calendar year in which elected." The club forbade transferring memberships. Individuals who withdrew agreed in advance to sell their memberships back to the club.

The Nile's by-laws bestowed on the club's board of governors the ability to "exclude from membership any active member or associate member who fails to comply with the reasonable and lawful requirement of the laws, rules and regulations" of the club. Exclusion from membership required that "ten days' notice has been given the offending member to attend a hearing before the Board of Governors." Finally, to maintain the family-friendly environment that the club sought to foster, the by-laws enabled the board of governors to "make such rules and regulations with respect to the means of determining the qualifications and the desirability of admitting applicants to membership as they may deem in the best interests of the Club."

Jet magazine, billed as the "Weekly Negro News Magazine," identified that the club's "stringent rules" aimed "to keep the club on a high level." Swimmers needed to "shower before entering the pool area" and "use foot baths before entering the pool." Rules prohibited liquor and gum and required women to wear bathing caps. To maintain cleanliness, Nile Club staff vacuumed the pool daily. They monitored behavior of visitors for "disorderly conduct" that resulted in all "miscreants to be ordered from the pool." The core of the club's membership, *Jet* said, came from Yeadon, but "many others are from Philadelphia." But there were some limitations. Lauretta Miller, whose family joined the club in July 1959, says, "At that time, it was very exclusive. Joining the club from outside of Yeadon required an invitation from a resident there."

The Mighty Nile

Jet contended that "the important point about the club is that it mirrors a higher income for Negroes" and "shows that they have a growing awareness of the social amenities." It was deemed important, at that time, that the Nile Swim Club "shows that Negroes are growing up and building facilities for themselves without feeling they are aiding segregation and thus denying themselves pleasures that others take for granted." *Jet* concluded that "Negroes in other cities are casting their eyes at the club and like what they see." The little swim club in Yeadon began to emerge as a "Mighty Nile," running through the center of the nation's civil rights discourse. The club became a symbol of Black independence and prosperity.

The Nile's high standards reflected those of the people living in Yeadon. Lamont Ferrell's family moved onto Orchard Street in the 1970s, purchasing their house for about $15,000. "That was a lot of money back then," Ferrell notes, especially for a family with six children. Shortly after, Ferrell's dad lost his job as a food concessions manager at the Philadelphia International Airport. He spent the next six months, with twenty years' managerial experience, looking for a job without success. "Those were hard times," Ferrell remembers. "We ate hot dogs every day because we couldn't afford anything else." While eating those hot dogs for dinner one evening, Ferrell's dad announced to his family, "The only way we're going to get out of this is to pick ourselves up by the bootstraps." He then declared his intent to start a business.

Ferrell laughs, "My mom thought he was crazy. None of us had any entrepreneurial skills, and my parents didn't go to college." Ferrell's dad did possess, however, plenty of experience in the food industry. That enabled him to recognize a need in the fast-food market, dominated by hamburgers at that time. Eating hot dogs each day, Ferrell's dad decided to turn "a negative into a positive" and open a new fast-food restaurant, Ferrell's Franks. Still thinking that her husband was crazy, Ferrell's mom identified the need for employees. Ferrell remembers his dad's response: "They are all sitting right here at the dinner table: my six sons."

They all soon went to work. By chance, a new shopping mall, The Gallery II, opened its doors in Philadelphia and needed vendors. "My dad and older brother Stephen somehow convinced the bank to give him a loan," Ferrell says, "and we opened our first Ferrell's Franks in 1983." The business took off. Ferrell's Franks soon opened stores at three more locations. Ferrell remembers, "My dad hired half of our neighborhood to work for him.

From left: Juana McCormick Berge, Jane Lewis Abbott, Pamela West, Melissa Jackson Robinson and Helen Puriefoy at the Nile in 1981. *Edith "Sugie" Dixon.*

He had something like twenty-five employees." A few years later, Ferrell's Franks garnered the City of Philadelphia's "Small Business of the Year" award. "That was great," Ferrell observes. "It changed our lives.

The Black professionals who lived there, through struggle, perseverance and hard work, managed to build a suburban oasis uncommon in the United States. They possessed great confidence and the resolve that their children would receive the opportunities that they had not. They built a swim club that anchored a community infused with a spirit of "can do." Even if White Yeadon maintained separation between the town's east and west, the Nile was equal, if not superior, to White segregationist swim clubs that refused to consider Black applicants. The Nile opened its doors to all.

Ericka Rumi Grant's mom, Shihomi Goto Grand, for example, frequented the Nile often, finding it after coming to the Philadelphia, successfully auditioning for the Pennsylvania Ballet, marrying and raising a family in Yeadon—all after leaving Japan. In speaking about her mother, Rumi Grant says that when she came to the United States, she "knew no English, but she learned from television." Rumi Grant remembers going to the Nile daily with her mom and little brother. She laughs, "You could never tell she was Japanese. If ever everybody in the room is Black, then she's Black. Everything that everybody else was doing, she wanted us to do too." At the pool, Rumi Grant recalls her mom feeling welcomed. She says, "Oh yeah, everybody loved her."

I Talk Right, Not White

Inside the club, there existed a tightknit community aligned with West Yeadon's values and dedicated to the pool's success. In its efforts to maintain high standards, however, the club contributed to a perception emerging among some Black folks elsewhere about West Yeadon and its denizens. In "Black and Well-to-Do," Andrea Lee wrote, "I find that in some circles Yeadon is a synonym for conservatism and complacency, a place famed as being the hunting-ground of the AAP (Afro-American Prince or Princess)." She says, "But I don't care. Yeadon was a great town to grow up in." Lee explained that Yeadon constituted "as solid a repository of American virtues and American flaws as any other close-knit suburban community; moreover, it had, and still has, its own peculiar flavor—a lively mixture of materialism, idealism, and ironic humor that prevents the minds of its children from stagnating."

Not everybody on the outside understood this. Wanda Reese laughs, "Yeah, we have family in Philly, and they would say, 'Oh, you think you're bougie,' y'know like stuck-up, better than everybody else." They might say, "You talk like a White girl, just dumb stuff like that." Lauretta Miller adds, "A lot of people, especially in the early days, thought that the Nile Swim Club was an elitist organization. And you can say what you want, it was. It was exclusive. A lot of people from Philadelphia thought it was bougie." When pledging his fraternity at Cheyney, Anthony Patterson Sr. says, "I was kind of ostracized a bit." He recalls, "They used to call me White boy because they said I talked White." He "always told them, no, I don't talk White, I talk right."

Deborah Robinson Stewart says that when elsewhere, she sometimes claimed to be from nearby West Philadelphia. Otherwise, "They would say, 'Oh, you're from Yeadon, we heard about Yeadon girls.'" She recalls thinking, "What does that even mean?" But Robinson Stewart understood: "Definitely throughout the area, there was this perception that Yeadon was bougie." Mark Miller remembers fondly the Nile Splash parties he attended as a teen. Open to all, they attracted many young people from Philadelphia. Everybody enjoyed meeting one another, but sometimes getting the attention of girls provoked attention. He remembers, "Sometimes the Philly guys would be like, 'You Yeadon guys think you are all of that.'" Mostly testosterone chest puffing, he says.

Lamont Ferrell notes, "We didn't think we were better than anyone else. We were just kids growing up." He recalls taking some chiding from cousins who visited from West Philadelphia who "would talk about little stuff that is silly like grass." But, he adds, "It's true. You go to West Philly, and most people have a porch and then a sidewalk. There is no front yard, so they didn't have grass." As kids, he says, "We just sort of took it all for granted." Others understood this, including Ferrell's old basketball teammate at Temple University Kevin Clifton, a native of nearby Darby, Yeadon High School's old basketball rival. Both played for legendary Philadelphia coach John Chaney at Temple.

Within a group text including Chaney's former players, Ferrell recalls Clifton poking fun at him about his Yeadon upbringing. He told the others in the chat group who are from outside the Philadelphia area that Ferrell grew up in a "country club." Clifton told the others of Yeadon, "First of all, they had the most beautiful women in the world. They had lawns, cars, backyards, even their very own Swim Club, a Black country club." Ferrell laughs and says, "He called Yeadon a Black Beverly Hills." He adds, "He was dead serious. And, you know, when consider it all from the outside looking in, I can see how some people might think that. Especially by the Nile—those are nice homes, single houses, not row homes." Ferrell says that he understands how somebody visiting West Yeadon might think, "Wow, yeah, this is like a Black Beverly Hills. I just thought it was funny when he said it."

Lisa Ivery adds, "It's been said about the Nile before that there is a certain complexion of people there, the light-skinned. [That] there is a certain look that you have to have to be a part of that club." Her reaction to that, she says, is, "What are you talking about?" Ivery explains, "I was there since I was a kid, and there were all shades of us there. There were all different types of people there." She continues, "There were schoolteachers there, others, my friend's dad worked for UPS, and as for the Jacksons, their dad was a police officer." Ivery says, "There was a real mix of people there; as for other people's perceptions, that's just what they were: perceptions." And as one who played travel field hockey and other sports, she remembers that when playing teams on Philadelphia's Main Line, "It all seemed like nothing compared to Bryn Mawr or Ardmore; we thought, 'Okay, we're not on their level.'" She says her brother would joke, "We're rolling up in our busted station wagon, and they're rollin' in style."

We Are Keeping Our Family Together

Jacquelynn Puriefoy-Brinkley, daughter of Carson Puriefoy, the Nile's first president, emphatically denies that the Nile promoted elitism. She says, "It was all about the community." She points to Anthony Patterson Sr. as an example. "We knew his father; everybody respected him and his family, knew about the situation. We welcomed them, even though they could not afford to pay." Patterson's dad, Reverend Isaac Newton Patterson III, attended the Nile Swim Club's opening in July 1959. He passed away seven years later, in October 1966, when Anthony remained a very young boy, the youngest of nineteen children, all with Isaac Patterson's longtime wife, the former Mary Jaynes.

While short, Reverend Patterson's life proved notable in his devotion to family and community. After serving as pastor of the Emmanuel AME Church, Philadelphia, and then the Bethel AME Church, Lansdowne, he became the pastor of the Mount Zion AME Church, Darby, before receiving appointment as the presiding elder of the Harrisburg District of the AME Church. The Patterson family resided on East Fairview Avenue in Yeadon, near the Nile Swim Club. The large house, with six bedrooms, afforded the Patterson family plenty of space. At the time of Reverend Patterson's passing, fourteen children, including Anthony, age three, remained in the house with their mom. And they were determined to keep it that way.

"At that time," Anthony says, "there was discussion about splitting us up. They didn't think my mother could take care of us, so the talk was about foster care." This proved unacceptable for the close-knit members of the Patterson family remaining. "My older brothers and sisters and my mom fought that," Anthony makes clear. "They said, 'No, we are keeping our family together.'" So, Anthony's mom went back to school, earned her general educational diploma (GED) and went to work at Fitzgerald Mercy Hospital. She started with day shift, but that proved untenable. According to Anthony, "She just got too many phone calls from either our house or the schools." So, she transferred to the nightshift, 11:00 p.m. to 7:00 a.m. That meant, Anthony recalls, "She got home at 7:00 a.m., woke us for school and made a quick breakfast. She made us dinner every day at 5:00 p.m., then she would go to bed until waking for work at 10:00 p.m. She did that for over twenty years."

Anthony's older siblings stepped up to help their mom with parental supervision, as did the Nile Swim Club. In addition to Anthony's dad, his two older brothers David and Horace attended the Nile's groundbreaking. The family supported the project from the onset the best it could, but it did not possess the financial resources to purchase a membership. While Reverend Patterson owned a printing business and a few properties, Anthony points out, "AME ministers did not make much money at that time." That did not exclude the Patterson children from becoming part of the Nile Swim Club's community. The club's management made that clear.

Anthony remembers, "In order for us to go to the club, because we could not afford memberships, they told us that if we came in and cleaned up, we'd get a burger, fries and could swim for the day." He laughs, "So, I used to go over there, pretty much whenever I wanted to go swimming. And that was every day in the summer." He explains, "I would go there to work first, maybe around the pool, but whatever the manager wanted, I did." When he completed his work, he swam and benefited from the guidance he received from onlookers, staff and lifeguards, always taking care to offer pointers and ensure the safety of all children in the water.

By 1962, the Swim Club's successful community building had enabled it to mount an expansion program. The *Philadelphia Tribune* reported on May 1, 1962, that the club cleared "two and a half acres of recently purchased ground." Four years later, on July 5, 1966, the *Tribune* observed that the Nile had "over five acres of usable ground, in addition to its Olympic-sized swimming pool." This enabled the club to accommodate one thousand people, including three hundred under a covered pavilion. By this time, the Nile could stage basketball, tennis, volleyball and badminton for its members. Meanwhile, the snack bar received an upgrade, now featuring a "Formica counter around the bar." Two ping-pong tables, designed and built by Booker Brown and Harold Wise, sat nearby.

Buzzing with Activities

The Nile accomplished its growth under changing leadership. On January 29, 1963, original president Carson Puriefoy stepped down from office, according to the *Philadelphia Tribune*, due to "pressing business commitments." Walter Sullivan, "expressing the views of the general membership, praised Puriefoy for aggressiveness and loyal leadership." An election between Byron F. Reed, a teacher at South Philadelphia High School, and Thomas Gary, the club's outgoing vice-president who worked as a government supervisor, resulted in Reed's election.

The Nile Swim Club enjoyed a banner year in 1963, welcoming a record attendance of more than one thousand members and guests to its Fifth Anniversary Celebration on Friday, July 12. As the first invitational affair in the club's history, the festivities included an Aquatic Show, led by Johnny Hines, through the arrangements of Ernest Coleburn. This, while utilizing the pool's deck as a stage, the *Philadelphia Tribune* said, "rendered a hilarious water show and gave a superb performance of the Spanish Flamenco Dance." The day also introduced to visitors the club's newly paved all-purpose play area. A few weeks after its anniversary bash, the club held its Hawaiian Fiesta, "so popular and so awaited" that it attracted more than five hundred guests.

The *Philadelphia Tribune* noted about Byron Reed that he "always has time to pass a pleasant word, flash a smile and give a good strong handshake. He has the progress of the Nile at heart." With that in mind, Reed stepped aside in 1964 for Thomas Gary, the club's former vice-president, to take over the presidency. This proved to be Gary's first stint as president, returning to the post years later. He remained devoted to the Swim Club's success throughout the course of his life. In 1965, according to the *Tribune*, Gary's leadership resulted in the club "buzzing with activities," the pool regularly "crowded with members and their guests." Of course, this included the always anticipated Hawaiian Fiesta, held that year on July 25 with music by Bennie Lyons.

Throughout the 1960s, the Nile Swim Club thrived. Following Gary's presidency, Raphael M. Coel took the helm in 1966. A decorated World War II veteran, Coel served in the U.S. Army Air Corps. After the war, he worked for the U.S. Postal Service before taking a job with Prudential Insurance Company of America. He became a district manager, one of six African Americans in the nation at the time to reach that level of management with Prudential. Moreover, according to the *Murray Ledger & Times*, Coel emerged as a "major force" in the civil rights movement, working closely with Cecil B. Moore, Judge A. Leon Higginbotham Jr., Judge Eugene H. Clarke Jr. and Dr. Martin Luther King Jr. He received numerous awards for distinguished service from the NAACP, the Southern Poverty Law Center, Hampton University and the Fair Housing Council for his work on equal housing.

Following Coel's tenure, which included strengthening the relationship between the Nile and the NAACP, Robert Cook assumed the presidency, guiding the club from the 1960s into a new decade. Cook welcomed new ideas about developing the club, according to the *Philadelphia Tribune*, inviting original member Henrietta Stukes to a board meeting on June 16, 1969,

Nile Swim Club banquet. *Nile Swim Club of Yeadon historical documents.*

as she "offered a number of suggestions for the improvement of the Swim Club." One thing remained consistent: the Nile continued to welcome outside groups of children. On June 22, 1969, the *Philadelphia Tribune* remarked that Audrey Brodie, chairperson of the Club Visitors committee, did a "splendid job." On that day alone, the club welcomed Boy Scout Troop 350, almost two hundred boys brought to the Nile in three buses, in addition to the Bible Class No. 10 of Union Baptist Church of Philadelphia.

A Level Playing Field

With such activity all season, the *Tribune* lamented in August that "Labor Day will bring the summer of fun to a close at the Nile Swim Club. The gate will once again close, and quietness will again fall upon the ears of those who enjoyed the splashing and squealing of voices at the Nile." When that day arrived, the *Tribune* observed that the "Nile Swim Club climaxed the season on a highly successful note." It "closed the swimming season on Labor Day with a capacity crowd on an ideal summer day." After more than a decade of operation, the Nile Swim Club had prospered. It attracted guests from throughout the region, providing hundreds of youths with the opportunity to swim. The club became a proud center of community for West Yeadon, one that symbolized independence and equality to its members. The son of an original member, Kenneth Earl Green says succinctly, "The Nile gave us a level playing field."

The pride this generated was reflected in the club's pristine maintenance, supervised from the outset by Booker Brown. In 1971, the *Philadelphia Tribune* dubbed him "Mr. Nile." Mark Miller, son of an original member, helped as a teen with the maintenance of the pool's grounds. He says that he can remember when they all got together to purchase the club's first riding mower. "Before that," he laughs, "we had like a hundred push mowers that we were all just pushing all over the place." So, he says, "We bought a used Cub Cadet from somebody up on the Main Line." He remembers, "When we brought that thing back, everybody was fighting to be the first one on it. Even the adults! They told us, 'It's a dangerous piece of equipment!'" But, as Miller stresses, "That thing was really important for the club, because before, it was a hundred push mowers that Mr. Brown had running around."

Kenneth Earl Green spent his childhood at the Nile. In an interview, he says, "Mr. Brown, he is one that needs to be talked about in all of this." Green explains, "He was a Black man who worked for Westinghouse as a supervisor. Back in the 1950s, that was unheard of, but he was that good." Green remembers, "He was the maintenance guy for the pool. And he taught me so much." Green started working at the Nile under Brown's tutelage at the age of thirteen. He did a little of everything, from painting to taking care of the pool's filtration system. "You can't go without saying," Green declares, "that Booker Brown kept the pool alive a lot of the time during the early years. Booker Brown was the man. He was always there, until he got too old to maintain it."

Water Safety First

Taking care of the club and all who ventured into the Nile's waters required the highest standards in maintenance and water safety. In 1968, the Nile Swim Club hired John Izzard Jr. to serve as its pool manager. His selection to serve in that role typifies the Swim Club's consistency in hiring qualified individuals to oversee water safety. In Izzard's case, he was a recent graduate of Cheyney University (then Cheyney State College) who majored in special education. A qualified instructor of outdoor sports, Izzard held Red Cross certification in lifesaving and in water safety. Such expertise in its managers and lifeguards ensured pool safety, the top priority.

Karen Hall Eskridge, a lifeguard around that time, remembers that visiting groups posed the greatest challenge for the guards. On the stand one day that the pool welcomed guests, Hall Eskridge says, "There was this guy, a teenager but a big guy, and went straight for the deep end." She said, "Hey, can you swim?" He said yes. She said that she needed to see it. He replied, "Well, you'll see me swim when I jump off the board." Off the board he went, and according to Hall Eskridge, "He just went straight to the bottom. I was like, 'Really?' So, I went in and pulled him out. I got him to the side, and one of the guys came over and helped. I was like, 'Dude?!'" That precipitated the lifeguards adopting a new rule that required guests to demonstrate their ability to swim prior to going into the deep end.

Timothy Spain, a former pool manager, cites an incident that occurred "that speaks to the dedication and the commitment" of the Nile Swim Club's staff. Spain lived a block and a half away from the pool, and one day he "was home mowing the lawn, or something." He looked up and saw a helicopter circling around, prompting him to question, "Why is that up there? What the hell is going on? I looked up again," and he realized, "That's over the pool. So, I went over there." He said that the staff did not get the chance to call him yet, "but we had a near drowning."

Spain says, "A child nearly drowned, but the quick thinking of the lifeguards, all juveniles at the time, they saved that child's life." Spain remembers, "I was never so proud and afraid in my life. I could not imagine a child dying at the pool while I was the manager." He says, "But it went the way it was supposed to go. And we got accolades, because of the swift action taken by the staff. I couldn't take any credit for that, but they did a wonderful job." Owing to the dedication and training of the Swim Club staff, Spain adds, "those kinds of incidents have been few and far between."

YOU CAN SWIM RIGHT HERE

In the 1970s, the Nile Swim continued to prosper, based on the dedication of management and staff and the continued guidance of original members.

In 1972, Norman T. Miller, an original bondholder, assumed the club's presidency by election to replace Robert Cook. The Nile Swim Club's new president, in the tradition of the ones who filled the post previously, proved to be a civil rights activist. A graduate of Darby High, Miller went on to earn a bachelor's degree at Cheyney and a master's degree at Glassboro State (now Rowan University).

Two years prior to assuming the Nile's presidency, Miller challenged the Lower Merion School District's contention that it received no qualified African American applicants to interview for the position of guidance counselor. His challenge proved successful, resulting in an interview process that made him the first Black guidance counselor at Harriton High School in Bryn Mawr, Pennsylvania.

As for Cook, the *Philadelphia Tribune* reported that he "was praised for the remarkable leadership he provided to the Nile for three years." Elected board members included incorporators and past club presidents Carson Puriefoy and Raphael Coel, along with "Mr. Nile," Booker Brown. The leadership continued its active social agenda, hosting a ball on April 8, 1972, at the Twentieth Century Club in Lansdowne. The night paid homage to Robert Cook and his wife, Odessa, while featuring entertainment provided by Swinging Freddie and the Freeloaders. The band returned to the Nile in July for the club's Clam Bake and Dance. The Swim Club continued to maintain its high-water mark through the 1970s.

The Nile welcomed groups like the Philadelphia chapter of the Tuskegee Alumni Association at annual splash parties at the pool. During one of these, the Tuskegee alumni, students and prospective students gathered at the Nile, the *Tribune* observed, "where everyone was in a festive mood." Those in attendance spent "a relaxing day eating, swimming, sunbathing, taking pictures, playing tennis, table games and just relaxing." While the "city's pulse has slowed down" in August, the *Tribune* noted that "there is still plenty of life at alfresco events for which the Nile Swim Club of Yeadon is famous."

Lisa Ivery says, "There used to be a lot of groups that came in." She clarifies, "They used to come from other states like Maryland, in the big Greyhound buses." These constituted family reunions and other kinds of gatherings. Ivery laughs, "And you know me, I'm there by noon, have my space and I'm doing my thing. Then all of a sudden, there would be all of these people." She remembers, "As members, when they all came in, we'd always ask each other, 'Who are all of these people at our pool?'" Ivery adds, "We didn't know at that time, as kids, [that] to the African American community, the Nile was a legendary place to come."

From left: Hugh Dixon, Kevin from Paschall and John Realer, with Dawn Puriefoy in the back at the Nile in the 1970s. *Bernard Ariel Harris.*

To inaugurate its twentieth season in 1978, the club staged a parade on Memorial Day. The route extended a mile in length through the borough, with the procession led, from Church Lane and Bailey Road to the Swim Club at Union and Lincoln Avenues, by youth groups such as the Boy and Girl Scouts. According to the *Philadelphia Tribune*, the parade resulted in Yeadon "filled with the sounds of triumphant drums and heralding bugles" and acted in "symbolically representing the 'Kick-off' grand opening of the Nile Swim Club's summer season." Club president Stanley Linder cited the parade as an appropriate celebration of the "sole Black swim and recreation club in the area."

The parade proved a fitting tribute, but it served another purpose. The club's membership had seen a decline—while at the beginning of the decade it stood in the hundreds, by the end of the 1970s it had declined to 130. Club organizers sought to use the parade as a recruiting tool. Parade organizer William Carey told the *Tribune*, "While skeptics question the benefits of membership, you don't have to drive eighty miles to Atlantic City for a dip in a cool pool." He declared, "You can do it right here." The $300 membership, said Linder, stood as a bargain. It covered only about half the expense of the maintenance and operational costs of the pool and the club's other facilities. After two decades of exalting on the high dive, the club entered a period of treading water that nearly resulted with it wallowing in the deep end. The reasons for this are many.

YEADON'S UNREST

Rough Waters

By the end of the 1970s, West Yeadon's baby boom years had come to an end. The kids who frolicked yearly at the Nile in the 1960s and early 1970s, the ones who also helped maintain the pool and guard its waters, went off to college and then followed their opportunities elsewhere. Andrea Lee recalled in "Black and Well-to-Do" that by this time, "Yeadon became a place where parents vied with one another to produce tidbits about surgeon daughters and M.B.A. sons." And those parents, the founders and original members of the Nile, at the height of their careers in the early 1960s, grew older and began to pass away. The pool began to occupy a sort of intergeneration vacuum. Lisa Ivery, who frequented the pool in the 1980s, says, "Our generation went there, but nobody really thought about what it took to run it. That understanding wasn't really passed down."

The Swim Club's decline transpired as Yeadon became increasingly Black. This occurred due to West Yeadon's success as a Black suburb along with the widespread fame of the Nile. In the 1960s, Yeadon's Black population doubled; practically all of them lived in West Yeadon, but some began to live on the east side's western edge. This continued, resulting in Yeadon's Black population jumping to nearly two thousand by the end of the 1970s. By the 2000s, Yeadon's population had become 80 percent Black. As that happened, the racial détente of the old days held by the Mason-Dixon line provided by Church Lane shattered. Yeadon erupted in racial tension that, at times, resulted in intimidation and violence in opposing integration.

Racial tensions in Yeadon first surfaced in November 1967, centered on, as the *Philadelphia Tribune* reported, "Ten Negro middle-class suburban families" who became "dissatisfied with the living conditions in their Yeadon Arms apartments." As a result, the apartment complex, located at 600 Yeadon Avenue, on the far edge of the West End's Black bubble, faced a rent strike. It involved ten families who occupied the thirteen-apartment complex, nine Black and one White. The others, all White, did not join the strike. The owner, John Logan, asserted, "Only the Negroes are making the complaints." He added, "They are not on a rent strike. They are delinquent."

The striking tenants submitted their monthly rent to the National Fair Housing Association, which placed it in escrow and turned it over to the constable's office. The organization's director, William Mimms, utilized this tactic to prevent the owner from following through on his threat to send "in the constable to evict everyone." According to Mimms, the complaints involved leaky ceilings and the lack of a lock on the building's front entrance. He said that when the tenants "complained to the owner, they were told to fix the ceilings themselves." A striking tenant who spoke to the *Tribune* and requested anonymity said, "Since the apartment became integrated, the owner has fallen down in maintaining it." She saw this as in attempt to "perpetuate the myth that when Negroes move in, the neighborhood deteriorates." She and the others stood "determined not to allow that to happen."

On December 30, 1967, the *Tribune* announced that the strike was over. It observed that "the war of words…moved to the conference table last week where a settlement, at least for the time being, was negotiated." Logan, the owner, agreed to make several repairs that included ceiling work, new locks, regular appliance inspections and weather stripping. One of the tenants remarked, "These places don't deteriorate. The landlords just stop providing the service they formerly provided the tenants when the places were all white." This proved to be the first of an ongoing series of conflicts between Black tenants increasingly moving into previously all-White apartment complexes in Yeadon and their White landlords. Parkview Court apartments, situated in a predominantly White part of Yeadon, became a site of contention for the next decade.

Tired of Compromise

It all began in 1969 when James Cook and his wife and son applied for an apartment at the complex. Cook, a former member of the U.S. Marine Corps who served in the Korean War, worked as a foreman with a maintenance supply company on nearby Haverford Avenue. He wanted to move out of Philadelphia to be nearer to his workplace and so his seven-year-old son could take advantage of the opportunities that suburban Yeadon afforded. Parkview Courts rejected the Cook family's application. Donald T. Guiney, the building's general manager, offered to the *Philadelphia Tribune*, "We don't allow families in who have children under 16. That's all there is to it." After a "few random phone calls" to the complex, however, the *Tribune* learned that "dozens of families" there had small children, "including a small number of Negro families."

Cook filed a complaint of racial bias with the Pennsylvania Human Relations Committee (HRC). He explained, "I'm tired of the black man having to compromise." When he came back from Korea "after serving as a Marine," Cook said, "I came back home and had to ride in the back of a bus." And that, he clarified, "was a sickening feeling." Cook accused the Parkview complex of accepting only Black applicants to live there whom it perceived as conforming to a certain mold. He told the *Tribune*, "I personally feel that they just don't want any Negroes in there who are not professional people." Based on Cook's complaint, the HRC investigated and affirmed that "many of the families in Parkview have children under 14." Still, the commission "shelved" the investigation, citing internal personnel issues.

The affair left Cook irate. He said, "Either they think this is a case of discrimination or it is not. They think I'm going to tire and give up this fight, but they're wrong." Cook blamed the HRC for complacently abetting systemic race-based housing discrimination. He said, "This is why so many black people don't even bother reporting racial discrimination. Lots of landlords know that they can get around the Human Relations Commission. This is why they do this to us." Within a decade, while its surrounding community remained largely White, Parkview became predominantly Black. By 1978, according to the *Philadelphia Tribune*, the complex had become referred to by both the "general Yeadon community and Parkview residents" as "Black view," the "Yeadon Projects" or the "Sophisticated Ghetto."

Between April 1977 and June 1978, Parkview experienced five building fires. Among its tenants, this created "an atmosphere of frustration and concern." The fires, they contended, stemmed from neglect. The complex lacked both adequate maintenance and security. The *Tribune* reported on March 14, 1978, that the "front entrance to one of the buildings was easily accessible," while a basement storage area "had been visibly vandalized." Yet management, according to some tenants, proved unresponsive to all grievances. One observer blamed the tenants. Wayne Beverly complained, "People who really can't afford the rent move in from low income areas; with them they bring their [bad] habits." It all resulted in the Parkview changing ownership in 1978. This development, the *Tribune* reported, resulted in changing the complex from "deplorable to livable."

We Just Want to Live in Peace

The drama at Parkview transpired as Yeadon experienced unaccustomed racial strife. Yeadon's Black population, one that steadily increased during the 1970s, pressed across the borough's long-standing Mason-Dixon line. Black families began to purchase houses on the eastern side of town, which had remained predominantly White for decades. But during that time, as word spread about Yeadon's Black suburban enclave, the West End of Yeadon ran out of space. In addition, attitudes of those moving in had shifted. On February 26, 1987, the *Philadelphia Inquirer* observed, "Unlike their predecessors who migrated mostly from Philadelphia, many of the blacks in the newest influx were reared in nearby [areas] and worked in nonprofessional jobs." These individuals proved "not quite as prepared to accept what amounted to de facto segregation in housing."

That included some who grew up in West Yeadon. Jerome and Rosalind Johnson moved into the Cobbs Creek area of East Yeadon in 1974. Rosalind, a West Yeadon native and Philadelphia teacher, told the *Inquirer*, "I wanted to live in an integrated community." She compared growing up in West Yeadon to living in West Philadelphia in that she had little contact with Whites outside of attending school. Another who shared that view, Juanita Russell, moved to West Yeadon in 1971 and then left for East Yeadon in 1983. An owner of a Philadelphia beauty salon, Russell opened up a new shop on Yeadon's Church Lane.

In June 1978, the *Philadelphia Tribune* spoke with Janet Gore, an East Yeadon transplant "whose property was vandalized" the previous summer. About that, she said, "I had fewer problems out of white folks when I lived in Mississippi." At the time, Gore owned "the only visible Black business in Yeadon," a grocery store located at Wycomb Avenue and Providence Road. That corner, she said, had become "notorious for Black/white youth confrontations." She placed the blame for the escalating tension at the intersection of race and class. She explained, "The Blacks who are buying homes in Yeadon are better (financially) than the poor whites who don't want them there." She added, "We just want to live in peace."

Peace proved elusive. In February 1977, the *Philadelphia Tribune* reported that a group of White men abducted, robbed, tortured and shot Roland Conyers, a Black Yeadon resident, while walking down Lansdowne Avenue on his way to work. Conyers's attackers held him for nearly six hours, during which he "was pistol whipped, cursed, stabbed twice with a butcher knife and shot twice in the buttocks." They then dumped him in a park outside nearby Media, where police found him and took him to Tri-County Hospital.

According to the *Tribune*, the incident sparked "a number of calls complaining about the treatment Blacks endure in Yeadon." They claimed that attacks like the one Conyers endured "happen all the time." Callers asserted to the newspaper that "Blacks in that community are regularly intimidated and provoked by whites and the police are apathetic." It noted that a "recurring theme of the callers was that the attacks were aimed at forcing Blacks to move out of the community." The evidence supported this, revealing a pattern of intimidation and violence against Black people venturing into East Yeadon to reside.

In May 1976, Jacqueline did move from her East Yeadon home on Fern Street after somebody threw a firebomb onto her front porch. At about the same time, Clara Johnson moved into another house in East Yeadon. Soon after, she found all the windows in the house broken and a fire in the garage. The attacks continued. Sharon and Leonardo Littlejohn moved to Bullock Street, on an all-White block, in April 1978. From the time they moved in through mid-June, vandals shattered their windows on four occasions. They additionally splattered paint on their garage wall.

Sharon Littlejohn, seven months pregnant, told the *Philadelphia Tribune*, "I doubt I'd want to raise my children in an atmosphere like this." The Littlejohns, however, refused to move. This resulted from the real estate company's refusal to return the Littlejohns their $10,000 settlement costs. Michael Pole, manager of Carr Realtors, told the *Tribune* that his company considered itself "not responsible for compensating the family." He added that "since settlement was made, they are the property owners."

So, the Littlejohns purchased iron bars for security. Sharon explained to the *Tribune*, "I'm not giving up this house at a loss." Yeadon officials attempted to diffuse the situation and console the young couple. Mayor Nicholas D'Alessandro and other officials, including Dr. William Harris, Yeadon Community Relations chair, visited the couple to "assure that the violence would stop." Harris told the *Philadelphia Tribune*, "More whites are vandalized and harassed than Blacks." He continued, "But the reasoning and motivation is different. The Littlejohns' problem," Harris said, "has obvious racial overtones—it's ugly, regardless of the causation." Harris called it all "a pitiful situation."

Sharon Littlejohn agreed. But she took little solace in how officials framed the incident. Harris commented, "A fearful man is a dangerous animal." He detected that fear of integration ran rampant among some Yeadon Whites. They "just have to learn to live in integrated neighborhoods." He called their unwillingness to do so the problem's root. He attributed the vandalism to "kids, carrying out the wishes and desires of their parents." Sharon Littlejohn observed in response, "The police keep saying it's kids, it's kids, but that's no consolation. Our windows are still broken," she added, "and we have to pay."

Fighting the Status Quo

As some Whites acted to stop Yeadon's neighborhoods on the east side from becoming racially integrated, others fought against the creation of a community park, adjacent to the Nile Swim Club. The location, identified as the Sullivan tract, occupied eight and a half acres of land at Union and Lincoln Avenue. Creating a recreational space there constituted a "ten-year dream" for Stanley Linder, elected as the first Black council president in the history of Yeadon. Under Linder's leadership, the Yeadon West End Civic Association began working to transform the Sullivan tract into a green space in 1968. Linder told the *Philadelphia Tribune* that the land, long "an area dump for trash and garbage," constituted an "eyesore and health hazard" for the residents of West Yeadon. He said, "In the summer, it got so bad that rats used to run out the dump to the street and get hit by cars."

Elected to Yeadon's Borough Council in 1974, Linder served as the vice-principal of Vare Jr. High School in Philadelphia. After the borough proved unable to provide funds to transform the Sullivan tract into a "viable community space," Linder sought outside help. Planning began in 1976 after the project received funding from Housing and Urban Development

(HUD). Additional money came from the Bureau of Outdoor Recreation and Project 700,000. Construction began in 1977 and concluded one year later. The opposition throughout the process proved vehement and racially charged. Linder called those opposed to the project "jealous, ignorant and biased." He accused two of his colleagues on the Borough Council, fellow Democrats John Spina and Lee Burleson, of leading "racist white residents and opportunists" for "financial gain." He cited their interest in selling "the land to a developer to build expensive homes."

Spina fired back at Lindner, saying that he "forgets he was elected for all of Yeadon and not just 'his section.'" He and Burleson said that Linder, not them, sought to make the project a racial issue, "pitting Black residents against white." They insisted that their concerns stemmed not from racism, but from questions about "how Yeadon residents would pay for the upkeep of the recreational area later."

Linder held his ground, suggesting, "If that piece of ground was in the white section it would have been built years ago." Opposition in this case, he contended, stemmed from the resentment of some Whites "about spending so much money" on a facility that "they felt white kids would not be able to use." While White Yeadon boasted "more than 100 acres of park land," Linder noted, "there is no such area in the Black section."

Neither side appeared to listen to the other, and the issue escalated already heightened racist behavior. The *Philadelphia Tribune* reported on the groundbreaking ceremony for the new park in September 1977. One day later, vandals hit a Black-owned business in Yeadon, writing hate speech on one side of the store and "KKK" on the other. All the writing appeared in big red letters. Days later, a Black mom received a death threat in the mail. Again signed by the KKK, it threatened the lives of both her and her three children.

At the time, Robert "Bob" Bogle served as president of the West Yeadon Civic Association. A media executive, Bogle received appointment to preside over the National Newspaper Publishers Association in 1991. Two years later, *Ebony* magazine named him as one of America's most influential Black Americans. Commenting to the *Tribune* about the racial strife in Yeadon in 1977, Bogle indicated that Yeadon's Black residents believed that the acts "were committed by vandals from nearby white communities."

Bogle also pointed out that all the incidents occurred against Black folks, and Yeadon employed only one Black police officer. A kid in Yeadon at the time, Lamont Ferrell laughs, "Of course, Mr. Jackson! Everybody knew Mr. Jackson—he was the only Black cop! His sons, Tommy and Mark, went to school with me. They lived right around the corner."

No longer on the Borough Council, Stanley Linder joined Bogle and the West Yeadon Civic Association in calling for systemic changes, ones that empowered and protected Yeadon's growing Black population. After Linder stepped down from his council position in 1977, there was no Black representation on Yeadon's Borough Council. Linder stood as the first, and the only, African American to hold a seat. In 1978, nearly three thousand Black people lived in Yeadon, and they lacked any representation. This owed to an outdated charter that called for an at-large general election to fill council seats.

That scenario meant that Yeadon's Black areas, by then numbering three, including the Parkview Apartment complex, found themselves consistently outvoted. Council representative of Yeadon's Third Precinct Harry Porter told the *Philadelphia Tribune* that fair representation was overdue. He observed, "This is what you call deep politics," ones that enabled the "powers that be" in "preserving the status quo." For decades, the status quo in Yeadon meant relative racial tranquility. That no longer prevailed. As a result, Yeadon officials shifted their focus from teenage delinquency to unscrupulous realtors. The scrutiny proved warranted.

Great White Exodus

When the Littlejohns moved into their new home on Bullock Street in April 1978, according to the *Philadelphia Tribune*, "the neighborhood was flooded with brochures from a Galaxy Realtor." These requested residents to "sell their homes while the property value was still high." Shortly after, realtor Rick Sedio went up and down the block informing Bullock Street's White residents that a Black family had recently moved onto their block. Then came taped phone messages to the Littlejohns' neighbors that "stressed now is the best time to sell, before the home values drop." As it turns out, this did not prove to be Yeadon's initial experience with vandalism, realtor scare tactics and blockbusting.

The *Philadelphia Tribune* observed about Yeadon, "Ride down any street in the predominantly white section and the presence of sale signs are eminent as the shrubbery and flower beds which decorate these east side homes." A resident of West Yeadon remarked, "Whites are running scared. They are selling the homes like hotcakes." The individual concluded, "In a few years, Yeadon will be an extension of West Philly." Wracked by racial violence and intimidation, Yeadon now faced a "Great White Exodus," one that officials thought was provoked by individuals seeking economic gain. Reverend Paul Sorchek, a member of Yeadon's Community Relations Committee, called it all "artificially induced by realtors."

The U.S. Department of Justice investigated in Yeadon the previous summer after "several homeowners were harassed from racial motivations." Carl Gabel of the Justice Department explained to the *Tribune* that the incidents in Yeadon violated the 1968 Fair Housing Act, which prohibited individuals from selling their homes because of "entry or perspective entry of a minority person." In addition to the Justice Department, the Pennsylvania Human Relations Commission launched an investigation into the events in Yeadon. It reported receiving from the town a "substantial number of complaints."

Meanwhile, Yeadon's Community Relations chairman, Dr. William Harris, urged area residents to make the Littlejohns feel welcome. He said, "They probably feel alone and afraid and they should know that community is concerned." That concern prompted the Yeadon Borough Council to act. This stoked more controversy. On May 27, 1978, the *Philadelphia Tribune* reported that Yeadon's Borough Council attempted to pass Ordinance 1025. Intended for "esthetic reasons," according to council president Samuel Carr, the ordinance banned the display of "For Sale" signs.

Residents reacted strongly. They called its purported rationale a "smoke screen." Harry Porter, a resident of Providence Road, said, "I think this ordinance is being introduced for other reasons, but the Council does not have the guts or the fortitude to admit why." Ordinance 1025 stipulated that "no signs, billboards of any nature whatsoever advertising 'for sale,' 'for rent,' 'sold,'...be displayed on any residential property." It warned, "The posting of such signs" constitutes "a public nuisance," which will result in the property owner standing "subject to penalty."

Another Providence Road resident, Reverend Allen Roberts, told the council members, "You are wrong." He asked, "Who gave you the authority to say that an individual cannot post signs on a property that he rightfully owns?" Calling the proposed ordinance a violation of "free expression," Roberts warned, "I will circulate petitions to try my damnedest to prevent this ordinance from passing." An attorney from elsewhere in Delaware County, Barry Dozor, agreed with Roberts. He said the ordinance's passage would constitute "thumbing your nose at the law." Moreover, he suggested that it "will cause racial disharmony and dissension." Council member William Cumby informed Dozor, "I don't appreciate an outsider telling us what to do." After tabling the ordinance for further consideration, the council passed it, in revised form, at the next meeting in June.

In June, Yeadon Borough Council passed Ordinance 1025 by a five-to-one vote. It incorporated feedback that council members received at the previous meeting. Borough solicitor Roy DeCaro cited the revised ordinance as "more directed to unscrupulous realtors," while serving to "protect rather than prohibit the residents." The amended version specified as prohibited "certain activities relative to solicitation and sale of real estate." It targeted any display of signs "or any device representing that property is available for inspection, sale, lease or rent when in fact it is not." The ordinance forbade the "creation of incidents designed to create 'panic selling.'" It carried a maximum penalty for violations of $300 and thirty days in prison. "If anything is constitutional," DeCaro told the *Philadelphia Tribune*, "this is."

Sensitive Areas

James J. Pace, chair of the Delaware County Board of Realtors, worried that blaming realtors proved misleading. He said, "The problem is not unscrupulous realtors, it's unscrupulous individuals who use whatever they can to make a buck." He added, "We do police our realtors and are willing to hear cases of alleged foul play." Still, Pace found the racial steering, a practice of showing prospective buyers only select properties of all available, that had transpired in Yeadon as immoral. Pace indicated that he found "no fault" with the enforcement of the ordinance in racially "sensitive areas," recognizing them as "possibly tension-causing."

At the end of July, the *Tribune* noted, "Perhaps it is too soon to evaluate the effects of the enforced ordinance, but East Yeadon is quiet." There existed, it said, "little opposition from residents." The affected area, formerly all White, had as its bounds Church Lane on the east; Yeadon Avenue, Rundale Avenue and Duncan Street on the west; Whitby Avenue on the north; and Cobbs Creek Parkway on the south. The "sensitive area" received its boundaries from meetings between Yeadon's all-White Borough Council and the ten-member biracial Community Relations Committee, which contained five Black and five White members. Community Relations Committee chair Dr. William Harris said, "No, we don't want Yeadon to be an all-white community, but we don't want it to be all-black either."

Reverend Paul Sorcek, Harris's colleague on the Community Relations Committee, additionally sought to diffuse charges that the creation of a "sensitive zone" abetted rather than hindered racial steering. He explained to the *Tribune*, "There might be some people who applaud our efforts for racial reasons" but assured that "our committee is concerned about the exploitative efforts of real estate people." Marking a "sensitive area," he said, aimed only to curtail "panic selling in the affected area." He asserted that the committee stood "ready to stand by our decision" and suggested that "[t]here has to be a balance between individual rights and community rights." He recognized the effort not as a "cure-all for the white exodus and racial steering" but as "only one step towards a solution."

Some in West Yeadon, however, were skeptical. They saw the issue as one that transcended the act of displaying signs. Thirty-year West Yeadon resident Harry Porter suggested that the ordinance aimed to restore Yeadon's long-standing status of de facto segregation. He noted that the new law "passed by an all-white council, is merely an attempt to keep Blacks out of the predominantly white section. Many Blacks oppose the ordinance," as he told the *Tribune*, "but have chosen not to take a public stand." Yeadon Community Relations chair Dr. William Harris disagreed, saying, "Blacks should be allowed to move wherever they want."

Harris insisted that the ordinance did not constitute an attempt to keep Black people out of East Yeadon. Instead, it sought to stop "the unnatural movement of whites away and the influx of Blacks into the area," which Harris posited "will ultimately create a 'Black ghetto.'" Another West Yeadon resident pointed out that the ordinance "won't change attitudes. Whites who don't want to live with Blacks will move regardless."

We Have Those Stories

This proved prophetic. White flight went on unabated. Yeadon's Black population reached nearly 40 percent by the end of the 1980s and stood in 2020 at almost 90 percent. Throughout that time, racial tensions lessened, but they hardly disappeared. For example, Lamont Ferrell remembers routinely experiencing "drive-by"s as a teenager in the early 1980s while walking back home with his teammates from basketball practice through the predominantly White part of Yeadon. He says, "Nobody was shooting back then. They would just throw out the 'N-word' and drive by. Half the time we didn't understand what they were saying." On one occasion, they sought to make their message clear.

"So, on this particular day," Ferrell says, "some guy yells at us from a car, 'Get the hell out of the street.'" They drove slowly, close enough to reach out of the car and push Ferrell's friend Michael Joshua. This prompted a response, Ferrell recalls. "We yelled something back. And they turned around, bunch of White guys." And it dawned on Ferrell and his buddies as they came closer, "These weren't even high school kids. They looked like grown men. Probably nineteen or twenty, but definitely not high school age." The teenagers stood their ground. It resulted in Ferrell's buddy Michael getting into a fight with one of their tormentors. Ferrell marvels, "Michael got the best of him. And he was only fifteen. I'll never forget that." All that came next proved equally memorable.

Ferrell and his friends started running. But as Ferrell notes, "It was a long run back to our side of town." They made it back, only to ask, "My God, what just happened?" As they talked about it, Ferrell remembers, "It was like a movie. We looked up to see a pick-up truck coming down our street. And there were like ten White guys in the back." This resulted in more running, directly to Ferrell's house. He laughs at the memory. "I pushed open the door, and the only thing I yelled was 'White boys! White boys! White boys!'" The truck emptied, with its occupants spilling out and attempting to enter Ferrell's house. Ferrell remembers them pushing on the door while Ferrell and Joshua pushed back.

That's when, as Ferrell remembers, "My dad came down. He was a big guy, probably 250 pounds with muscles. He just busted up the crowd, put them in step." Meanwhile, neighbors had called the police, and they arrived, including Officer Frasier, whose daughter went to school with Ferrell and his friends. "We knew him," Ferrell says, "and other cops came with him." This calmed everything down. "But that is definitely a memory," Ferrell says. "I'll never forget that. Never." Ferrell remembers another incident from that time, one he did not witness but learned about from his friend Michael.

According to Ferrell, Michael Joshua emerged from the 7-Eleven convenience store one day, "the one right around the corner from Orchard." He saw a group of White guys blocking the sidewalk and thought, "I'll just cross the street and walk around them." The only problem, he found quickly, was that there another group occupied that corner too. So, he just kept walking. As he made his way through the group, one of the guys, drinking milk, dumped the carton over Joshua's head. Ferrell says, "So, then they got into it." But vastly outnumbered, wisely, this time Joshua ran. About those times, Ferrell says, "We had a great time growing up in Yeadon, but we have those stories. It's all just how we lived and what we dealt with." He adds, "We just kept moving forward, kept going the best we could."

THE BEST WE CAN

For Ferrell and his friends, that meant spending as much time as they could at the Nile Swim Club. They did so on day passes and by the invitation of members because they could not afford the membership fee. This proved increasingly common, even as Yeadon's Black population steadily expanded. Some of the newcomers saw the club as a relic of the past, a product of a community that proved out of touch with their concerns. In July 1978, amid the ordinance debate, one Black Yeadon resident told the *Philadelphia Tribune*, "West Yeadon Blacks don't react unless their front yard is on fire." He described people in West Yeadon as "too middle-class and too unconcerned." The *Tribune* commented that while "the predominantly white east section is confronted with racial instability…stable, affluent, predominantly Black west end remains complacently quiet."

A decade later, on February 26, 1987, the *Philadelphia Inquirer* ran a story titled "The Times of Yeadon's Black Enclave," which chronicled Yeadon's changing racial and economic composition. It observed, "More blue-collar blacks have moved in." As a result, "The black community once almost exclusively lived in the western portion of Yeadon, but now many blacks are living in eastern Yeadon as well."

One of them, Reverend Allen Roberts, moved from nearby Darby to Yeadon and became a Borough Council member. He told the *Inquirer* that "many of the less affluential new residents such as himself thought the older black generation of Yeadon residents were living in ivory towers." He found them "cool to newcomers." David Warrington, a retired history teacher, added about West Yeadon residents, "Those people thought they came over on the Mayflower."

The *Inquirer* noted that longtime residents of West Yeadon remained undeterred by the perception held by some of the newcomers. They stood committed, according to the *Inquirer*, "to retain the tradition that once put their black enclave in the national spotlight as an example of racial harmony and black economic success." Original Nile Swim Club member Audrey M. Brodie added, "We'll carry on the best we can."

And that they did, but it proved a struggle at times. One that members now recall as the club's "Dark Days." Even so, the pool remained a magnet for Black kids throughout the region. Timothy Spain grew up in North Philadelphia and received an invite from a friend to one of the Nile's Splash parties in the early 1980s. He remembers it as "a wonderful experience for a kid from north Philly, to come out to this Black suburban pool."

Meanwhile, in Yeadon, the Nile circulated a notice: "Some of our original members are no longer as young as they used to be, so there is room for new young families to join and carry on the dreams." But this proved easier said than done. The Nile Swim Club's high standards, adopted by the founders to ensure the club's success and to demonstrate the ability of Black folks to create a swim club that rivaled White-only clubs like the Yeadon Swim Club, began to cause difficulties in recruiting new members.

Original member Lauretta Miller observes, "When the complexion of our community began to change," from professional to working class, many of Yeadon's new Black residents "still had that attitude." That is, she says, they thought, "I'm not going to join the Nile Swim Club. You didn't want me then, why would you want me now?" As a result, Miller points out, "The membership and the interest began to fall tremendously. The Nile started to fail." This transpired as the club approached a historical milestone, one that brought outside recognition.

THE WORST OF TIMES, THE BEST OF TIMES

A Significant Part of Our History

In 1989, the Nile Swim Club commemorated its thirtieth anniversary. The club's founders gathered at the pool, where, according to the *Philadelphia Inquirer*, "dressed up for the occasion," they "sipped wine, nibbled on cheese and told stories about the conflict that led to the club's founding and the problems they encountered along the way." A week earlier, the Nile's founders had gathered at Philadelphia's Afro American Historical and Cultural Museum. There they donated memorabilia from the club's early days, including the shovel Zoe Mask used in the groundbreaking. She additionally gave the museum the scissors she used to cut the ribbon at the club's opening in 1959. Philadelphia mayor Wilson Goode, in attendance, called the items "a significant part of our history."

The occasion at the museum included a reception attended by almost two hundred people, including Goode and other dignitaries, such as U.S. Attorney Edward S.G. Dennis. A 1973 graduate of the University of Pennsylvania's Law School, Dennis became the first Black assistant attorney general of the Criminal Division by appointment from President Ronald Reagan in 1988. The cases that he supervised while acting in that capacity included the indictment of General Manuel Noriega of Panama. He and the others at the reception for the Nile's founders listened to Rowena Stewart, the museum's executive director, locate the Swim Club in its historical context.

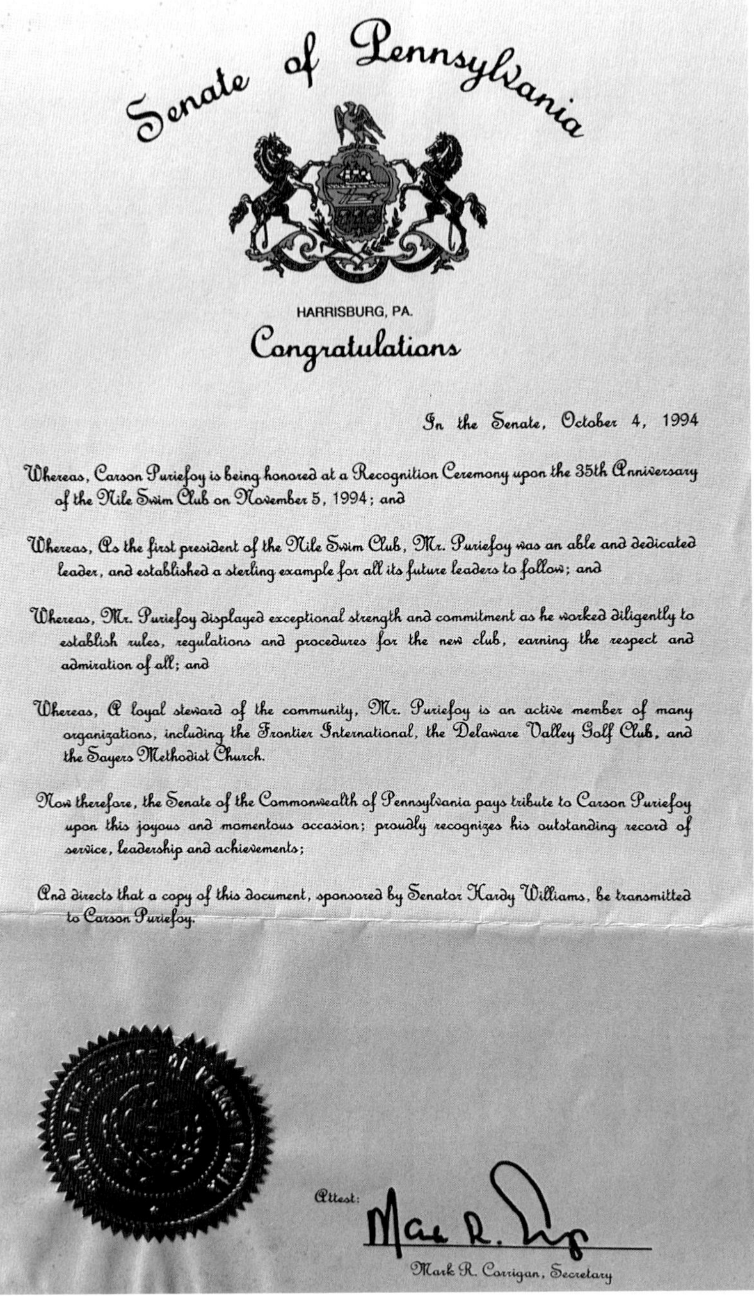

Senate of Pennsylvania

HARRISBURG, PA.

Congratulations

In the Senate, October 4, 1994

Whereas, Carson Puriefoy is being honored at a Recognition Ceremony upon the 35th Anniversary of the Nile Swim Club on November 5, 1994; and

Whereas, As the first president of the Nile Swim Club, Mr. Puriefoy was an able and dedicated leader, and established a sterling example for all its future leaders to follow; and

Whereas, Mr. Puriefoy displayed exceptional strength and commitment as he worked diligently to establish rules, regulations and procedures for the new club, earning the respect and admiration of all; and

Whereas, A loyal steward of the community, Mr. Puriefoy is an active member of many organizations, including the Frontier International, the Delaware Valley Golf Club, and the Sayers Methodist Church.

Now therefore, the Senate of the Commonwealth of Pennsylvania pays tribute to Carson Puriefoy upon this joyous and momentous occasion; proudly recognizes his outstanding record of service, leadership and achievements;

And directs that a copy of this document, sponsored by Senator Hardy Williams, be transmitted to Carson Puriefoy.

Attest:

Mark R. Corrigan, Secretary

Pennsylvania State Senate recognition of Nile Swim Club founder Carson Puriefoy. *Nile Swim Club of Yeadon historical documents.*

She said, "If you were part of the Nile Swim Club, then you were part of the struggle." She emphasized, "And we need future generations to know the story of your struggle."

At the event's toast, founder Robert Mask took the opportunity to remind everybody that in addition to becoming familiar with the Nile's history, the club needed young people to tend to it in the present. Mask announced his desire to "turn the pool over, lock stock and barrel to those people who were kids back then." He said that this would ensure "the older people can come back, look and enjoy." Many of those kids, however, lived elsewhere. This constituted another challenge, created, in some ways, by the success of the Nile and its founders in raising children who mirrored the ambitions and talents of their parents. As the *Philadelphia Inquirer* observed in 1987, "The children of the original settlers are successful professionals living in large cities through the world."

Won't Give Up

Lamont Ferrell, one of those who left, became a successful screenwriter and producer. He says that he and others talk about that, the large number of individuals from their generation who became successful in a wide variety of professions. He says, "We all say that it was literally in the water. We grew up in it and we drank it." That enabled them, Ferrell observes, "to believe that we could do anything that we wanted to do. Our parents instilled that in us." He notes that Yeadon provided a unique environment for its Black children. "Unfortunately, in America, for many African Americans, when you grow up and you don't see a lot of people who look like you who are doing positive things, well, you don't believe that you can do them." In Yeadon, that proved not the case.

Ferrell cites his own experience, one watching his dad get laid off from his longtime job at the Philadelphia International Airport and then start a business "out of nothing, literally." That business, Ferrell's Franks, became successful in Philadelphia's largest shopping mall. Ferrell says, "Then people go downtown, and they see our name on the marquee, they say, 'That's Mr. Ferrell! Wow! Maybe I could start my own business!'" And besides Ferrell's dad, children in Yeadon saw every day their parents come home from work, "and they had that briefcase." Ferrell recalls, "You wanted to do that. You wanted to be successful in something, and I think that pushed a lot of us.

I mean every day we would see these people, teachers, lawyers, doctors, coming home from work and cutting their grass."

Of course, not everybody left. Some became quite successful and remained in Yeadon. But as Lisa Ivery remembers, they knew nothing about running a pool. She says, "My generation went to the Nile daily and had fun. But that's how we saw it; nobody really thought about what it took to run the place, and it wasn't passed down." But the problem, according to former pool manager Timothy Spain, came down to the question of what to pass down.

Spain says, "My understanding of it, until recently, [was that] with the Nile's leadership there were always two sides. And you had to be on one of the sides." On one side, Spain explains, people wanted to "do things the ways they'd always been doing them." People on the other side, however, sought to bring about changes, ones that aligned with Yeadon's changing complexion.

Ivery says, "There was a lot of infighting going on, people not agreeing with each other. There was a lot of stuff going on." The standoff resulted in the Nile's leadership striving for years to keep the club above water. "The Nile went from this place that was bustling and that people wanted to get into," Lisa Ivery remembers, "to a place that you drive by and think, 'I don't even want to go there; it looks so run-down." According to Ivery, this resulted from "not handling the business of the Nile." She explains, "People weren't taking care of it in a true sense, you know, figuring out how to keep it going, to make necessary changes and updates so people had the desire to come in." Ivery adds, "But there were also positive people around, on the board, ones who kept pushing, who wouldn't give up on the club."

TROUBLED WATERS

Bill Mellix Jr. attended the pool's opening as a child in 1959. As the Nile struggled decades later, he assumed a position on the club's board. Thinking back, Mellix Jr. reflects on "one of the concerns, or issues, that I had was that everybody on the board was old." He remembers telling others on the Nile's board, "We need to get some young folks in here, get some young thinking. We're all still thinking in the 1960s and 1970s." To start that process, Mellix Jr. invited a friend's son, Jason, "an intelligent young man," to join the board. Mellix Jr. recalls taking him to a board meeting.

And, of course, Mellix Jr. says, "It was a typical board meeting, where everybody was fighting and fussing and hollering at one another." Once things calmed, Mellix Jr. introduced Jason, the son of original Nile members, as a potential board member. Mellix Jr. laughs, "Jason said, 'I don't think I want to be on this board,' and he walked out." Mellix Jr. told Jason that he did the right thing. He also thinks that it served as sort of a wake-up call for his fellow board members. Mellix Jr. explains, "I think it made people stop and think for a second. 'We just ran this young man out because of our actions, our stupidity.'"

Kenneth Earl Green remembers walking into this environment. As a kid, he helped care for the pool under Booker Brown. He left Yeadon and became a property manager in New York City. When he came back, others told him of the pool's dire straits and invited him to join a meeting. Green remembers arriving there to find "everybody screaming at one another." He laughs, "And I said, 'I can volunteer my services. That's all I said.'"

This led Green to doing the pool's maintenance and becoming the club's vice-president. When the president resigned, Green recalls looking around the room and saying, "Guess that means I'm now president." Of that role, Green says simply, "I didn't like it." He explains, "I'd hold meetings and hear, 'You're not doing parliamentary procedure right.'" He remembers thinking, "I've got more important things to worry about than parliamentary procedure. But that's where we were."

A club member beginning in 1990, Gwendolyn Brown became one who helped the Nile negotiate the rough waters that it encountered. A transplant from Pittsburgh, Brown found the club when she sought a place for her child to learn how to swim. She says it reminded her of a Black pool that her family frequented in Pittsburgh, but the Nile "was Black owned and operated, which really appealed to me." She became a member, paying dues for nearly thirty years while serving in a variety of leadership positions, including board member, membership secretary, vice-president and president.

Brown served as Green's vice-president, and he says, "Nobody talked about her, but she was instrumental in the life of the pool." He notes, "She's the one who recruited me to volunteer back in 2012. She was president before me, and she's the one who took over the presidency after me." Green asserts, "Gwen is the one who held us down."

Brown first served as president of the Nile from 2003 to 2005. When handed the keys to the club by Zelda Mincey, the Nile's outgoing president, Brown thought to herself, "What have I gotten myself into?" She says, "I often have those same feelings to this date." In 2003, according to Brown, "the Nile did not have a penny in the bank." Its bank account overdrawn, the Nile owed the phone company, the electric company and the water company. Its pool supplier, Delaware Valley Pool, had taken the club to court due to its inability to pay its outstanding bill for pool supplies.

Brown immediately went to work. She started by visiting Delaware Valley Pool and successfully negotiated a payment plan. She recalls that the company proved sympathetic to the club's plight and worked with her and others at the club to get the pool open. She says, "They taught me everything about the operation and maintenance of a pool." She adds, "To this date, I am very grateful for that."

Fundraising came next. It began with Jacquelynn Puriefoy-Brinkley, daughter of the club's first president, Carson Puriefoy, an original member who remained involved with the pool.

Puriefoy-Brinkley personally loaned the club $1,500 to make an initial payment to Delaware Valley Pool, which the Nile later paid back. The pool company dropped its court case, and Brown negotiated payment plans with the phone company and the other utility providers that the club owed. She and her team also secured funds from Yeadon Borough to provide youth swim programs. According to Brown, these ranged from $8,000 to $13,000 per year. Fundraising efforts included everything from bake sales to clam bakes.

At the club, Brown made "safety, cleanliness/sanitation, sound money management and customer service top priorities." New members received welcome letters and informational handbooks. With his background in regulatory compliance and standards, Brown and his team developed an operation manual to enable the club to function "consistently and efficiently." This included necessary repair work, including the full replacement of the pipes under the pool's surrounding concrete decking.

Efforts also involved the creation of an orientation session and water safety training for daycare camp providers. This provided an additional layer of safety for the children who came to the Nile from the more than a dozen area day camps that the Nile serviced. Brown coordinated this effort from 2003 to 2016. It generated nearly $20,000 per season, a sum Brown says "helped us significantly."

Striving to Replicate History

As the Nile's outreach increased, its membership dwindled. With a peak of five hundred members during the 1960s and 1970s, membership now hovered around one hundred, dropping to as few as seventy. The programming and fundraising helped stabilize operations, but the club's taxes proved problematic. Brown says that when she assumed the presidency, the Nile's taxes stood two years in arrears. "To my understanding," Brown explains, "the two years in arrears had been going on prior to me even joining the club." The previous president, Zelda Mincey, however, stressed to Brown the importance of paying the current tax bill. Otherwise, due to the arrears, the Nile would go to sheriff's sale. Under Brown, the club paid its tax bill every year, while making "efforts to pay and/or resolve the back tax issue with all diligence."

In 2006, founding member Thomas Gary became the Nile's president. He had previously served as the club's president in 1964. This appeared fitting, as the Nile celebrated its fiftieth anniversary in 2008. That summer, the *Philadelphia Inquirer* cited the Nile as using the occasion of its anniversary to "bring black families together and to reach out to the community." Gary said, "Family is a very strong unifier at the Nile." He continued, "This is just trying to get together some of the old-timers and new-timers." He then added, "It's going to be just a hoopla time for all."

All the club's work to right its operations resulted in memberships climbing to more than two hundred. This prompted planning for expansion. Gary hoped to turn the Nile into a "three-floor, year-round facility." Projected to cost $5 million, the plan included the addition of an eighteen-hole miniature golf course, a volleyball court, a banquet hall and fine dining facilities. Gary indicated that the club raised $300,000 to date and sought to supplement that sum with state grants.

The club's plans generated excitement in the Nile's community. It reinvigorated the connection between past and present for the Swim Club's members and others. On February 11, 2008, the *Philadelphia Daily News* reported "Big Plans for a Venerable Swim Club." Nile Swim Club steering committee member A. Bruce Crawley told reporter Stephanie Farr, "They did something 50 years ago that deserves to be replicated by this new generation of African American residents and the leadership of this region."

Crawley alluded to the Swim Club's newly anointed "ambassadors," a group including people such as State Senator Anthony Hardy Williams and J. Whyatt Mondesire, president of the Philadelphia chapter of the

NAACP. They enlisted, Crawley said, to "replicate what happened 50 years ago." To do this, Crawley explained, the "ambassadors" received charge to identify "potential members from their network and corporate resources for the Nile."

Jacquelynn Puriefoy-Brinkley served as Gary's vice-president and also sat on the Yeadon Borough Council. Nearly ten years earlier, as council president, she oversaw the shuttering of the Yeadon Swim Club over its inability to pay taxes. That situation developed, according to Puriefoy-Brinkley, largely because of the Yeadon Swim Club's refusal to integrate, even as it faced shutting its doors. She says, "My life experiences have taught me that you are so much richer when you are exposed to different people."

People who "isolate themselves or their children," Puriefoy-Brinkley offers, "are missing out on what is so important in life." The Nile's history inspired her planning with Gary and the others to expand. She told the *Daily News*, "We were very ambitious about it, and I think some of that ambition came from the early days of the club."

By this time, only one original founder remained alive, ninety-three-year-old Robert Mask. He continued to stress the central role in the pool's construction played by his wife, Zoe. He called her the "main instigator" of the project. He noted, "My wife was one of those persons people would use the slang term 'feisty' to describe." As it turned out, just as all again appeared to go swimmingly once again, the Nile Swim Club's community soon found that it needed to rekindle the feistiness displayed by its founders. While fundraising initially proceeded accordingly, enabling planners to set construction to start within a year, America's economy collapsed. The 2008 recession drained the pool of potential donors.

A Community Commitment

Two years later, the *Philadelphia Inquirer* reported about the Nile's expansion, "The project has been suspended." Thomas Gary passed away the previous year, and Darrell Henderson now presided over the Nile. About the Swim Club's challenges in the new economy, Henderson said, "People aren't looking to pay a membership for a swim club when they are trying to survive." The Swim Club also found itself in a struggle to survive. Membership dipped to below one hundred. Moreover, the aborted project, one that would have constituted the first green development in Delaware County, brought about unintended tax consequences. These stemmed from the club's early history and threatened to close the Nile down permanently.

The new tax problem derived from the Nile's expansion in the early 1960s. That land factored into the new development plan, and the Swim Club needed to present copies of its deed to move the process forward. According to Gwendolyn Brown, "It was learned that we never obtained the deed for the additional land." So, Brown "took off a day of work" to research "Yeadon Borough hand-written minutes" to confirm that the sale took place. This succeeded. She found that the Nile paid $6,000 to acquire the land from Yeadon Borough.

Brown says, "The various payments were in the written Yeadon Borough Council meeting records, which verified that the additional land had been paid in fully by the Nile Swim Club." It proved enough to prompt the borough to issue a "special resolution to give the Nile Swim Club the deed to the property." All appeared well until "the deed was conveyed," and then "the property taxes shot through the roof." Serious tax delinquency resulted that, as Brown remembers, "nearly caused the Nile to be lost to sheriff sales."

On September 30, 2012, the *Philadelphia Inquirer* reported, "Pioneering PA Swim Club Files for bankruptcy." Nile president Darrell Henderson told reporter Kristin E. Holmes, "We just couldn't turn around that kind of money." He explained, "So that we wouldn't lose the property, we filed for bankruptcy." That "kind of money," according to the *Inquirer*, consisted of $90,049 in delinquent taxes through 2009, with an additional $36,768 tax bill for the year. Most of this money the club owed to the William Penn School District.

Gwendolyn Brown says that the school district "did nothing to support us." She adds that they "refused to work with us. We presented several different payment plan proposals prepared by our lawyers, and none were accepted." The *Inquirer* noted that Yeadon officials stood "committed to finding a way to preserve the pool." Borough Council president Asher Kemp Jr. asserted that the pool's "historic significance enriches our community." Club members felt the same.

Frances Gilbert, a twenty-five-year member of the Nile, told the *Inquirer*, "The Nile means an awful lot. We should strive to do whatever we can to support it and make sure it remains open." Jacquelynn Puriefoy-Brinkley remained someone who did just that. Even as membership dipped to seventy, a historical low, Puriefoy-Brinkley remained confident that the work of her father and his friends would endure. She observed, "There is a commitment to the Nile that is unlike any commitment to anything I've ever seen."

Lisa Nelson Haynes cited the reason for this. She said, "This is me. This is my history." The granddaughter of original members, Nelson Haynes, says, "This teaches us that we came from something and can do for ourselves." Puriefoy-Brinkley adds, "It's a painful time and it's going to be hard, but I think we're going to be fine."

To ensure that was the case, members and friends once again rallied with fundraising efforts. They recognized the need, however, to boost membership. In July 2012, Swim Club president Barbara Willis explained to the *Philadelphia Inquirer*, "We need to at least double our membership to feel good, not great, about our situation." She emphasized, "We don't deny anyone," and cited the club's current White and Latino members. "We're the last ones standing," Willis noted, "we need to keep it going."

Willis soon stepped down from the presidency, however, and Darrell Henderson, a Yeadon native who acted as the general manager of the Philadelphia International Film Festival and Market, assumed the position. Described as someone with a "positive spirit" and a "contagious smile," Henderson appeared ideal for the job. Talk remained focused on how best to attract families back to the club. Kia Puriefoy, Puriefoy-Brinkley's niece, noted the Nile's need for improvements. She said, "These buildings haven't been refurbished in God knows when." She described the club's grounds as "wonderful" but added, "you need something on them. They at least need to build a snack bar."

To generate funds to do so, member Tammi Forbes suggested reaching out to previous members no longer in Yeadon. "With so many of our people doing such great things," she offered, "they need to just buy a membership." In whatever way, noted twenty-five-year member Roosevelt Harper, "We have to keep this going." He observed, "The pool means everything. It's a sense of pride." On that point, all agreed. The Swim Club's historical significance appeared clear to everybody. Restoring its past prominence, however, remained challenging.

Team Nile

Through the summer of 2012, with membership at an all-time low, the club possessed only enough resources to maintain daily operations. In May 2013, Puriefoy-Brinkley acknowledged to the *Philadelphia Inquirer* that "there wasn't much thinking about what we need to do to secure the future." This meant that the Nile proved unable to meet the payment schedule developed in court through the bankruptcy proceedings. As the *Inquirer* stated, "In the fall, the situation appeared bleak." It then got worse. President Darrell Henderson died in his sleep on December 5, 2021, at the age of fifty-nine. With the sheriff sale scheduled later in December, all seemed lost.

For the second time in three years, however, "a last-minute reprieve saved the club." As it turned out, somebody incorrectly recorded a parcel of borough property as belonging to the club. This brought the sale to a halt to, once again, straighten out a deed issue. Longtime friends who grew up at the club Dr. Bernard Harris, Kenneth Green and Richard Barnes saw an opportunity and assumed club leadership. With another friend, Arnold Coleman, the group met informally, brainstormed and dubbed themselves "Team Nile."

Team Nile took its ideas to Nile Club leadership. After the close call in December, that constituted "a governing body of the current active leadership." Gwendolyn Brown, co-chair of the interim governance committee at this time, says that this arrangement resulted because "the newly elected board of governors had been proven to be an illegally constructed board." According to Brown, the board possessed "many dysfunctions and was dissolved by the vote of the active membership." Until electing new officers and a board of governors in April 2013, current active membership assumed management of the club's affairs in order to "ensure the club's survival."

These centered on a "business-oriented strategy" and convinced the Nile to install Harris as president, Green as vice-president and Barnes as treasurer. Board member Gretchen T. Allen told the *Inquirer*, "For the first time in a while, we see guys coming back and rolling up their sleeves." They went to work immediately. They scheduled fundraisers and began networking with members of banking, business and philanthropic communities.

The group also reached out to local colleges, seeking help from students in exchange for the opportunity to learn and earn credits. They identified that facility improvements required "bartering, negotiating and partnering." Green hoped that "we can generate enough interest." He added, "This is history to us. We are here because we love this place." The new plan sounded good, but its execution proved difficult. Internal politics soon led Harris to resign the presidency.

Green recalls that during a meeting, Harris unexpectedly announced, "As of tomorrow, I will no longer be running the pool. I quit as president. He threw his papers on the table and walked out." Green laughs, "He just decided to take his ball and go home. It was a trip, but he is a really good guy." This left Green as the next one up. He assumed the presidency but clarifies, "I really didn't want the job. I was happy being vice-president and doing the maintenance because that is what I'm used to." Still, he gave it his best. He shared his approach with the *Philadelphia Tribune* in June 2014, saying that he "is trying to get back to where our roots are. We need the participation of people."

With Gwendolyn Brown as Green's vice-president, the reconstituted "Team Nile" launched new fundraising efforts while also working to institute a competitive swim team and a basketball league. The club doubled its membership from the previous year's 70 to 140. The taxes remained the club's greatest problem, up from $90,049 in 2009 to $134,000 in 2013. According to the *Tribune*, these included school, borough and county back taxes. "Team Nile," which now included Jacquelynn Puriefoy-Brinkley as treasurer, remained optimistic.

Puriefoy-Brinkley informed the *Tribune* that she felt, "It's like starting over again." She pledged, "We are going to take it to the next level." Richard Barnes agreed. He said his dad, a founding member, "would be grinning from ear to ear to see the club's existence and the ongoing effort to maintain this facility." He added, "We feel we're reaching out to the right people in order to proceed."

Day in Court

In 2016, Gwendolyn Brown assumed the Nile's presidency for the second time. She says that the Nile continued to possess "the burden of the unpaid taxes." This now amounted to $250,000. Like previous administrations of the club, Brown's paid current taxes, approximately $30,000 per year, and "did our best to appeal to the William Penn School District." District officials remained unresponsive. According to Brown, "We had no choice but to file bankruptcy again." This constituted the third time that the club had done so in less than ten years. This required permission.

Brown remembers, "We could only get a hearing for the last day." The club's venerable history suddenly looked to many as all that might remain. The Nile's present, and its future, came down to a day in court. If not successful, this time, no reprieve existed. The club faced dismantling and sale. Outsiders were already maneuvering to get ahold of the site, with one plan existing for construction of a nursing home.

Brown says that members Barbara Johnson, Tuskegee veteran Ms. Alma Bailey and Gretchen Allen accompanied her to the courthouse on the appointed day. She remembers the group sitting in court recognizing "that we were on the verge of losing the Nile Swim Club."

When it came time, Brown testified about "our increased membership, that we paid our current taxes and had the support of Yeadon Borough." She adds, "The lawyers from the William Penn School District and Delaware County Tax Office did all they could to convince the judge not to let us file." They claimed, she recalls, that "we would never be able to pay the arrears and ongoing taxes." Inexplicably, the Nile's courtroom opposition stood unprepared. Brown says, "They were unable to inform the judge about how much we owed." This contrasted with Brown's group, which "had our records in our hands to show that we had paid our current taxes." Brown states, "That saved us. The judge, in his mercy, allowed us to file bankruptcy once again." For Brown and the others from the Nile, "It was a very emotional moment, one that I will never forget."

Once again, the Nile had new life. When Brown's presidency ended, Christopher B. Sample, Philadelphia City Council member Kenyatta Johnson's longtime chief of staff, became president. The community rallied to save the Nile, contributing about $40,000 through a crowdfunding campaign. Lisa Ivery, part of a newly constituted board of younger members that became instrumental in the club's resurrection, told the *Philadelphia Inquirer* confidently, "No, we're not going to lose the club." She made that clear to the William Penn School Board. She recalls addressing the board at a meeting. She said, "You cannot say goodbye to the Nile Swim Club over these taxes. I'm sorry, you cannot."

Ivery's passion sprang from spending much of her childhood at the Nile. The club offered a welcoming community, unlike the Lansdowne Swim Club, which rejected her mother's application to join. The Iverys became fixtures at the Nile, with Lisa's mother, Ellen, serving on the board and becoming its recording secretary. Ellen Ivery worked diligently to help the Nile stave off bankruptcy, and now her daughter Lisa followed in her footsteps. She occupied a board seat and became its recording secretary.

Ivery pleaded the Nile's case. She told the school board, "We'll give swim lessons until we can't give swim lessons anymore. We are going to dig ourselves out of this, but we need an opportunity to get it together. We have a good team of people now, but you need to give us a chance." She continued, "Otherwise, your school board will be known as the ones to put the Nile Swim Club, the legendary Nile Swim Club, under. Do you want to be the ones responsible for us losing this historical place?" She explained to the board, "You should be helping to lift us up and help resolve these issues." This time, local officials vowed to help.

Chair of Delaware County Council John McBlain remarked, "They have a special place in Yeadon and indeed in the whole county." He said, "We want to be as flexible as possible and work with the Nile Swim Club." Another new addition to the Nile's board, Anthony Patterson Sr., asserted, "I will not see, I cannot see, the Nile Swim Club lost to sheriff's sale." He added, "I truly honor those founding families." Patterson and the club's leadership throughout demonstrated exactly that.

THE REST IS HISTORY

Patterson grew up near the Nile, the youngest of nineteen children, with his widowed mother and siblings. He went to the Swim Club daily, even though his family could not afford to join. His deceased dad, Reverend Isaac Newton Patterson III, attended the club's opening and possessed a stellar reputation in the community. Nile management allowed Anthony in to swim, let him grab a burger and some fries from the snack bar, in exchange for his help around the pool.

Patterson eagerly did whatever the Nile's staff needed. He learned how to swim at the pool, became proficient on the diving board and benefited from the mentorship he received from the Nile's staff. Patterson's time at the pool left a lasting impression as he went off to college and then began a successful career outside of Yeadon.

Patterson graduated from Cheyney University in the mid-1980s and took a job with Bell Atlantic. Mobile phones had just hit the market, and Patterson remembers cold calling physicians, carrying a phone in a briefcase that, he says, "must have weighed fifteen pounds." He told them, "This is the latest and greatest technology." He laughs, "The battery was bigger than the phone. It took up half the briefcase." Despite the unwieldy size of early phones, he remembers telling his brother Sam, then pursuing his MBA at Penn's Wharton School of business, "Sam, I think we should look at this. The cellphone business is going to be big."

Sam demurred, however, as he wanted to start his own business. With a job offer from IBM, a company that already employed two of his siblings, Sam told Anthony, "I think you better take that job at IBM." So he did. And he still needles his brother: "Had we pursued that opportunity, we'd be retired multimillionaires by now." He laughs, "But we did not, and the rest is history.

After a stint at IBM, Anthony Patterson Sr. began his own business, one that planned events and promoted concerts. This began as, while living in Delaware, Patterson noticed that everything shut down when DuPont closed at 5:00 p.m. With an aim to create networking events for African American professionals, Patterson began setting up social meetings at local restaurants that began regularly attracting more than four hundred people. This, along with his fraternity connections from Cheyney, led to Patterson orchestrating events such as homecoming concerts for regional HBCUs.

Patterson says, "I just started making money, y'know, doing that." His business, the Patterson Group, began booking "all those hot rap groups then, like Naughty By Nature." He recalls, "I started taking them around. Like they used to call it back in the day," he laughs, "the Chitlin circuit. I used to do the HBCU circuit." Recognizing the demand for live rap music, the Patterson Group worked out a deal with Pulsations Night Club in Philadelphia, promising to pack the place with college students on Monday nights. It delivered, bringing in acts such as Biggie Smalls and Wu-Tang Clan.

Patterson says, "That's the good news." The bad news entailed "folks acting crazy and tearing the place up. I had lots of insurance, but it was insane." Patterson remembers that one night "state troopers came in and ran everybody out of there." He remembers, "I had to run out of there with about $20,000." He says, "I paid the guys that performed, had security get me to my car. Then I sped out of there!" Some of the acts "got a little crazy," Patterson explains. "I got tired of that, so I joined by brother Sam's consulting firm." The business received minority contracts from businesses such as IBM and KPMG.

Sam Patterson's consulting business enjoyed great success, leading to a decision to become involved in real estate. Anthony Patterson Sr. says, "Sam was doing well and said that he wanted to start buying properties." This compelled Anthony to "reinvent myself again." He went back to school and earned his real estate license. He took over the company's property management, amassing more than one hundred properties under management. Patterson explains, "I mostly buy, sell and flip."

He also rents apartments. Patterson's office is in Broomall, Pennsylvania, but he manages properties throughout Pennsylvania, Delaware and New Jersey, coordinating a network that includes family members and fraternity brothers. Patterson says, "Anybody in this country who works twelve hours a day, seven days a week, well, there's a work ethic I admire. That's my motto." He soon took his philosophy back to the Nile Swim Club.

Patterson's path back to the Nile originated in his continued passion for event planning. Each year, Anthony and his wife staged a large New Year's Eve get together at their home for his family and friends. These began at 9:00 p.m., and "most times they would go until about 4:00 a.m., when the last of the Pattersons would leave." He recalls, "The last one I had, the last Patterson left at 6:00," he laughs. While the parties always proved to be a great success, the sheer number of people who came prompted Anthony to look for a larger venue. He immediately thought of the Nile Swim Club of Yeadon as a possibility.

We Will Not Lose This Pool

Thanksgivings with the Pattersons, a close-knit family, result in about one hundred people at the dinner table. Anthony Patterson Sr. needed a space, and he thought, "I'll take a look at the Nile." When he visited, he spoke with a few board members, including Lisa Ivery and Shawn Johnson. He says that they both said, "This place is a mess. Can you help us?" According to a 2020 article on the pool by the *Philadelphia Inquirer*, Patterson "had no idea until he returned two years ago, to scope out the club as a potential party site for his family, that this legendary oasis for the Black community was teetering on dissolution due to thousands of dollars in back taxes."

At that point, the bathrooms remained as they were when it opened in 1959. The pool's filters dated to the 1970s. Nile Club member Cliff "Brother" Brock wrote later in a newsletter about the Nile's state of disrepair at this time. He noted the club's $5,000 monthly water bill due to "broken pipes allowing the water to run like the Nile river in Africa." He explained that "guests were getting wood splinters from sitting on warped wood" and that many went home rather than use "the dilapidated locker rooms or bathrooms." Brock wrote, "With termite damaged wood and a collapsing roof, there appeared no light at the end of the tunnel."

Seeing the club's state prompted Anthony Patterson Sr. into action. He says that he told Ivery and the others, "We are not going to let this historic pool go away. The pool means too much to our community." Anthony Patterson Sr.'s reaction "was to call my brother Sam because he has the deepest pockets." Of course, he too grew up with the Nile and stood as equally determined as

Anthony to help. Anthony described the gravity of the club's situation to his brother and said, "Sam, we have got to do something about this."

Sam agreed. He placed a call to another Yeadon native, Mike Pearson, owner of Union Packaging. Pearson then reached out to Robert "Bob" Bogle, president of the *Philadelphia Tribune*, who, according to Anthony, "has the governor's ear." Progress proved immediate. Anthony reported back to the Nile's board, "Bob [Bogle] got us a stay. But we have to commit to paying these taxes." Anthony sought out a tax attorney to work out a payment plan and to negotiate an appropriate annual tax bill. For the $30,000 annually that the Nile then paid, it received no services. "They didn't even take our trash out," Anthony says.

As Anthony went to work on the taxes, his brother Sam and friend Mike Pearson delivered needed funds. Sam Patterson wrote a check for $50,000, and Pearson "went to his Foundation and came up with another forty-some thousand." This set Anthony and the Nile's leadership off and running. First, to fix the bathrooms. They brought in contractors to gut the bathroom and locker room facilities and also set about upgrading the pool. Fixing that stuff, they reasoned, offered chance to "start driving revenue up with increased membership."

According to Cliff "Brother" Brock, beginning in early winter, volunteers worked with a local landscaper to clear dead trees. He says, "We gave out firewood for free as a community service." In early spring, clubhouse renovations began. These included putting in a new concrete floor with decorative tiles. Brock explains, "We installed a new roof, gutter and drains" along with "new sinks, toilets, showers and outside siding." He offers, "We left no stone unturned, including new paint, flowers and plants."

Meanwhile, Anthony continued working on the taxes, successfully negotiating a lower annual tax bill, which was long overdue. Anthony says, "That was our highest bill, and we are only open three months." As the club began repairs and resolved the tax situation, it turned to recruiting new members. It accomplished this after Anthony did some homework. Anthony went on a tour of existing swim clubs in the area to learn about membership rates. He found that most charged from $500 to $600 per year. He thought, "That's a little high for our community."

Lisa Ivery, on the board during the dark days, came to the realization, "Everywhere you look in Yeadon there are Black people. That is who this club is made for, and they are not coming in. This just doesn't make any sense; everyone who lives in the town should have a membership." She continues, "If you think back to the founders and how they saw it, they said

A fresh coat of paint. Ola Osinupebi (*standing*) and Lateefah Patterson (*kneeling*). *Cliff "Brother" Brock.*

we can build this whole club with just a few Black folks in town." Ivery adds, "But if the whole town is full of Black folks, then what is the problem?" She adds, "We came up with offering free swim lessons. When you are in the worst position, that is when it is especially important to give back. People will embrace us if we just start giving."

The Nile set its membership at $300 per year, less expensive, given inflation, than it cost to join the pool in the 1960s. Within two years, club membership had increased from two hundred to more than one thousand. "That's when," Anthony says, "I knew we could pay our bills." It also allowed him and the others "to fix this place up." Anthony introduced the Nile to a business model, one that utilizes "multiple revenue streams." This translated into initiating a variety of initiatives, from "tree drives" to programs such as

No Child Will Drown in Our Town™. The Nile also orchestrates activities such as a basketball clinic and a tennis academy. Perhaps the most innovative is Jessie's Garden. Created by partnering with Nemours Children's Health, the effort features a one-thousand-square-foot garden on the Nile's grounds. It aims to promote gardening and healthy eating.

WORTH THE RISK

"Where we are today," Anthony Patterson Sr. notes, is rooted firmly in the club's origins. He says the Nile is about "pushing people to come in and make it a safe place." That is, he stresses, is the club's "first asset." Patterson explains, "When you come in these gates, for the kids and their parents, you don't have to worry about fighting, anybody acting crazy." He adds, "We pretty much control everything inside those gates, everything on those four and a half acres." Doing that, he says, means the club can be "very successful."

The Nile's days are tightly organized around activities, with swim lessons in the morning and other programs and events throughout the day, each day, all week during the summer season. About the Nile's resurgence, Patterson says, "With everything else going on in our community, we needed to make sure this place came back and became a safe haven for our children. I mean, with all the violence and madness going on, I said, these kids have got to go somewhere where they feel safe. And their parents can drop them off, and their parents can come here and relax and not deal with the craziness."

After all, Patterson notes, "Growing up there, I know what the Nile did for me, my family and friends. We knew we could go there, have fun, get something to eat and feel safe." He adds that the Nile Swim Club's founders "put up their mortgages to build this place in 1959, so we kids could swim here. They risked whatever they had to risk." Patterson makes clear, "I would risk whatever I had to risk to not lose this pool."

In 2020, the *Philadelphia Inquirer* reported that Philadelphia's public pools, along with most others, remained closed due to the Coronavirus. But, it identified, "not the Nile—and that is no small thing." The club even staged a Fourth of July fireworks show, "socially distanced of course." The *Inquirer* found the Nile's opening, despite the club's warranted uncertainty that "they would draw enough members in the middle of a pandemic to cover expenses," as refreshing. After all, the *Inquirer* noted, "This hallowed place in Yeadon nearly went out of business in 2018."

It did not. And now, during a global pandemic, the Nile opened its doors to the community, just as it always had. Reporter Maria Panaritis commented, "This club was born a fighter and remains a fighter—a model for us all during this most difficult year." The Nile Swim Club's history demonstrates this. The waters of the Nile refresh as they inspire.

Making Its Mark

In May 2021, the Nile Swim Club's historical significance received recognition from the Pennsylvania Historical and Museum Collection. Commission Chair Nancy Moses dedicated a marker near the front of the club that reads, "Opened in 1959, it [Nile Swim Club] is the nation's first private swim club owned and operated by African Americans. Led by three civic-minded families who were denied membership at the local swim club, community members united and purchased land for their own facility. Although the Nile is open to all, it has fostered and encouraged aquatic, civic, social and cultural opportunities that otherwise would not have been available to African Americans."

The marker resulted from the organizational efforts led by Bill Mellix Jr., one of the first to jump into the Nile's waters when the pool opened in 1959, and the Yeadon Borough Historical Commission. Mellix Jr. remains an active, instrumental member of the Nile's community. In supporting Mellix Jr.'s initiative to gain a historical marker, the eminent Charles L. Blockson, curator emeritus of the Charles L. Blockson Afro-American Collection at Temple University in Philadelphia, Pennsylvania, noted that "the founders of the Nile Swim Club made a bold step in self-determination." This resulted, he wrote, from their "awareness of the lack of opportunities and restrictions resulting in proportionately more deaths by drowning of African Americans."

The club's importance, Blockson asserted, resided not only in exhibiting "segregated recreation in a northern state" but also in showing how "African Americans countered racial discrimination by creating their own institutions and organizations." The Nile Swim Club, Blockson observed, "demonstrates African American agency during a period of racial injustice and discrimination. A state historical marker for the Nile Swim Club," Blockson concluded, "is long overdue."

Lori and Anthony Patterson Sr. in front of Nile Swim Club of Yeadon Historical Marker. *Anthony Patterson Sr.*

That day came on May 21, 2021. The *Philadelphia Tribune* reported, "Attendants fanned themselves and patted perspiration from their brows but seemed unbothered by the heat as they applauded the celebration of one of America's greatest achievements for African-American people and the legacy of those who refused to be denied the same privileges as whites because of discrimination." The dedication honored the past. Denise Stewart Swann, daughter of founder Elmer Stewart, said, "They wanted us to join a swim club but unfortunately we weren't able to join the pool that was in Yeadon at that time, so our parents, along with other friends and neighbors decided to do something about it and the rest is history."

That history included numerous strong women, including Zoe Mask, the one who pushed to create the Nile and then named it, and Elmer Stewart's wife, Florence, who proved instrumental behind the scenes. Denise's brother William "Bill" Stewart observed about the Nile's women, "They don't get the credit they deserve." Lisa Ivery observes, "At the end of the day, women get the work done. We do what we need to do, and we won't take no for an answer. We handle our business, and we keep things in order." She adds, "Just like Zoe Mask, it is less about 'What is my title?' and more like, 'Okay, this is what we're going to do.' This is the name of the club."

Nile president Anthony Patterson Sr. added, "We are proud of what we did here at the Nile. We are a proud heritage."

In addition to commemorating the club's history, though, the dedication was also an occasion to celebrate the present. One of the women who played a key role in preserving the club through its dark days, Lisa Ivery, told the *Tribune* that the Nile "is a place where you can learn to swim for free." She additionally identified the Nile's opportunities to participate in "skills and drills," join the basketball camp or tennis academy.

But she also noted that the Nile Swim Club remains "a place where you can come and just have a dip in the pool on a hot day and hang out and barbecue and bring your family and friends and just have a wonderful time." The Nile is the place "where the community can come together." Ivery adds, "We're trying to make the Nile part of everybody's culture, no matter what you look like, whatever your bank account is. Swimming is not an elitist thing." That community, which congregates at the Nile Swim Club, is formed of members united, rich in history, proud of the present, optimistic about the future and, always, welcoming to all.

REFERENCES

Oral History Interviews (December 2022–August 2023)

Andre Kenneth Andrews
Alma Bailey
Serrano Brown
Nita Dunham
Karen Hall Eskridge
Lamont Ferrell
Sa'ood Gibson
Ericka Rumi Grant
Kenneth Earl Green
Joe Harris
Lisa Ivery
Gabriel Johnson
Josie Jones
Bill (Billy) Mellix Jr.
Lauretta Miller
Mark Miller
Norman Miller
Latoya Monroe
Doris Fuller Moody
Lisa Nelson-Haynes
Rai Nelson

Anthony Patterson Sr.
Sam Patterson
William K. Pugh
Jacquelynn Puriefoy-Brinkley
Wanda Reese
Timothy Spain
Deborah Robinson Stewart
Levon Stewart
William "Bill" Stewart
Yvonne Burnley Studevan
Henrietta Stukes
Denise Stewart Swann
Florence Thompson
Kathleen Wainwright
Barbara Ann Johnson Williams

Periodicals

Ebony magazine
Jet magazine
New York Times
Philadelphia Daily News
Philadelphia Independent
Philadelphia Inquirer
Philadelphia Tribune

Documents

Nile Swim Club of Yeadon historical documents. Bill Mellix Jr. Collection.

Books and Articles

Brooks, Cheryl Woodruf. *Chicken Bone Beach: A Pictorial History of Atlantic City's Missouri Avenue Beach*. Mechanicsburg, PA: Sunbury Press, 2017.

Colquitt, Kevin. "The Power of the Nile Swim Club." Pool: A Social History of Segregation. Fairmont Water Works, 2022.

Dudziak, Mary. *Cold War Civil Rights: Race and the Image of American Democracy*. Princeton, NJ: Princeton University Press, 2011.

Gutman, Marta. "Race, Place, and Play: Robert Moses and the WPA Swimming Pools in New York City." *Journal of the Society of Architectural Historians* 67, no. 4 (December 2008): 532–61.

Hyser, Raymond M., and Dennis B. Downey. "'A Crooked Death': Coatesville, Pennsylvania and the Lynching of Zacharias Walker." *Pennsylvania History: A Journal of Mid-Atlantic Studies* 54, no. 2 (April 1987): 85–102.

Kibler, M. Alison, and Shanni Davidowitz. "'Our Color Won't Wash Off': The Desegregation of Swimming in Lancaster, Pennsylvania." *Journal of Civil and Human Rights* 2, no. 1 (Spring/Summer 2016): 3–32.

Kodosky, Robert J. *Tuskegee in Philadelphia: Rising to the Challenge*. Charleston, SC: The History Press, 2020.

Mills, C. Wright. *The Power Elite*. Oxford: Oxford University Press, 1956.

"Prejudice and Pride…The Story of the Nile." Nile Swim Club Historical Marker Proposal.

Rubeiro, Alyssa. "Under Two Flags: How Nancy Giddens Built Bridges Between Black and Puerto Rican Neighbors." *The Metropole: The Official Blog of the Urban History Association*. Pennsylvania State University.

Wainwright, Kathleen. *Summer in the City*. Diona N. Murray, illustrator. Middletown, DE: Willa's Tree Studios, 2021.

Wiltse, Jeff. *Contested Waters: A History of Swimming Pools in America*. Chapel Hill: University of North Carolina Press, 2009.

———. "Swimming Against Segregation: The Struggle to Desegregate." *Pennsylvania Legacies* 10, no. 2 (November 2010): 12–17.

Zinn, Howard. *A People's History of the United States: 1492–Present*. New York: Harper & Row, 1980.

Websites

Fairmount Water Works. "Pool: A Social History of Segregation." https://fairmountwaterworks.org/pool.

Goin' North: Stories from the First Great Migration to Philadelphia. https://goinnorth.org.

Persistent Racial/Ethnic Disparities in Fatal Unintentional Drowning Rates Among Persons Aged <29 Years, United States, 1999–2019. Centers for Disease Control and Prevention. https://www.cdc.gov/mmwr/volumes/70/wr/mm7024a1.htm.

ABOUT THE AUTHOR

Robert J. Kodosky received his PhD in American history from Temple University. He is a professor of history at West Chester University, where he teaches courses in American military and diplomatic history. His other books include *Construction Ahead: Making American History Since 1865* (Great River Learning, 2024), *Tuskegee in Philadelphia: Rising to the Challenge* (The History Press, 2020) and *Psychological Operations American Style: The Joint United States Public Affairs Office, Vietnam and Beyond* (Lexington, 2007). His contributions to other publications includes ones to the *Encyclopedia of Greater Philadelphia*.